Healing
Your Spine

Rebalance your Self
and Gain Access to your
Entire Life Force

Stefan Rippel

First published by O Books, 2008
O Books is an imprint of John Hunt Publishing Ltd., The Bothy, Deershot Lodge, Park Lane, Ropley, Hants, SO24 0BE, UK
office1@o-books.net
www.o-books.net

Distribution in:

UK and Europe
Orca Book Services
orders@orcabookservices.co.uk
Tel: 01202 665432 Fax: 01202 666219
Int. code (44)

USA and Canada
NBN
custserv@nbnbooks.com
Tel: 1 800 462 6420 Fax: 1 800 338 4550

Australia and New Zealand
Brumby Books
sales@brumbybooks.com.au
Tel: 61 3 9761 5535 Fax: 61 3 9761 7095

Far East (offices in Singapore, Thailand, Hong Kong, Taiwan)
Pansing Distribution Pte Ltd
kemal@pansing.com
Tel: 65 6319 9939 Fax: 65 6462 5761

South Africa
Alternative Books
altbook@peterhyde.co.za
Tel: 021 555 4027 Fax: 021 447 1430

Text copyright Stefan Rippel 2008

Design: Stuart Davies

ISBN: 978 1 84694 137 5

Printed by Chris Fowler International
www.chrisfowler.com

O Books operates a distinctive and ethical publishing philosophy in all areas of its business, from its global network of authors to production and worldwide distribution.
This book is produced on FSC certified stock, within ISO14001 standards. The printer plants sufficient trees each year through the Woodland Trust to absorb the level of emitted carbon in its production.

Healing
Your Spine

Rebalance your Self
and Gain Access to your
Entire Life Force

Stefan Rippel

BOOKS

Winchester, UK
Washington, USA

617.564/4702479

CONTENTS

Acknowledgement

First of all I want to thank my wife Magdalena for her patience and her enduring support which enabled me to write this book. I want to thank Anitha Kohs for reading; correcting and contributing occasionally her ideas on this topic. I thank Theresia Pieler for the great artwork she did on the illustrations and Miriam Karner for modelling for the photographs in the book.

My special thanks to Rosalyn L. Bruyere who set me on the path of healing.

Finally I want to thank all my clients and students for the trust they have in me and that I have the privilege of learning from my work with them.

Introduction

Four in five adults will experience back pain at some point in their lives, and most of these will suffer several recurrences of back pain. The luckier ones are affected only occasionally but those suffering from serious chronic restrictions are on the increase. The situation is getting worse as the population is ageing. But back pain is not exclusive to older people. It is a disorder which affects all ages and it indicates that something has lost its balance in the entire system of our body's functions, whether it occurs in a child, an adult or an old person.

Pain of any kind is first of all a warning sign. Whenever something goes wrong in our body we receive a signal in the form of pain. This signal is always given when we overstretch our physical capacities, for example, if we try to turn our right thumb outwards as far as possible with our left hand. Long before we really hurt ourselves by overstretching the joint capsule, we will be stopped by an intense sensation of instant pain. A similar mechanism is found in our spine but the pain there only occurs after extended periods of physical self abuse. Your body will tell you straight away that it does not like you sitting at the computer day in day out for hours and hours. It will make you feel uncomfortable in your neck and shoulders or occasionally it will give you a headache.

We should become more aware of the underlying causes for back pain of any kind. Unfortunately most of us lack a clear perception of ourselves at a physical level. Do you really have a clear picture of the shape of your body or do you just have a vague idea? Can you feel the middle joint of your right foot's third toe? Can you feel the two small joints between your fourth and fifth lumbar vertebra? Or do you feel your body only when it hurts somewhere? At this stage the need for increasing your self awareness becomes essential. There is no "expert" except yourself

1

at this crucial point to tell you how to live your life without harming yourself. The choice as to whether you waste your life in self destruction or develop it to its full potential is up to you.

Back pain is, of course, a physical sensation. But we have to take into consideration that the physical body is just one component of a whole self. There is also an emotional, a mental and a spiritual body and all of them have an equal importance and meaning. Many disorders of our physical body have their origin in an imbalance in the interaction between the different components of the whole Self, which can be understood in the sense that emotions can affect the physical body, as well as mental patterns. The impact may not be felt immediately; in many cases it is a long period of time before it manifests itself physically as a spine problem.

Here is an example of an emotional impact which can occur as a spine problem 25 years later. Imagine a healthy, open-hearted little boy around the age of three sitting on the floor in the living room playing with Matchbox cars. Usually his Daddy comes home from work around this time, and just as he does every day, the boy drops his toy and runs with wide-open arms towards his father to give him a welcome hug. Unfortunately Daddy has had a really bad day. Being angry and frustrated he does not reciprocate the affection. He turns away and addresses the boy with harsh words and shrugs him off with impatient gestures. This simple action has an enormous emotional impact on the child. His father's rejection shocks the boy because it happens without any obvious reasons to him.

Such an emotional injury initiates a negative program in the boy's subconsciousness. The physical gesture of his wide opened arms experienced the pain of being rejected by somebody he loves. If this is reinforced many times the boy will develop muscular patterns to protect himself from being emotionally injured again. Rooted in his subconscious mind, in the long run these patterns will restrict the flexibility of his skeletal muscles in the neck and shoulder areas. Muscles contract to avoid pain of any kind, whether emotional or physical. This is what muscles always do. This kind of conditioning leads to muscular rigidity, which in the long run will express itself physically as a body posture which causes back pain. Or worse, it will lead to tissue degeneration. This is because a state of permanent muscular tension disturbs the metabolism of muscles, cartilage and bone structures.

Back pain cannot be cured by psychological analysis alone, especially not in cases where severe symptoms have led to extreme physical pain. It cannot be cured by only treating the physical symptoms through medication or physiotherapy. These have no influence on the emotional traumas which often lie hidden deep below the surface. To cover both the somatic as well as the psychological needs at the same time, we have to find a link between all the elements involved. This connecting link must be part of the physical body, the emotional and the mental. The connecting link is vitality.

What is the difference between a rotting branch and a blooming one? Why does one person's tissue degenerate earlier and another person's much later? To find an answer to these questions we have to understand the concept of vitality. The only way to understand the meaning of vitality is to be aware and to experience consciously our own life energy. A mere explanation of the concept of vitality is a hopeless attempt. It is like someone attempting to define the taste of salt. No one will ever understand the taste of salt unless he has experienced it on his own tongue. In order to experience vitality we need to be as flexible as possible with our spine. If our spine is restricted in its mobility through pain, we will be restricted in our self perception as well. This vicious cycle can be broken by using our awareness to localise our restrictions in movement and to dissolve them through exercises. It will expand our ability to perceive our own vitality. The clue to finding the access to our original vitality is to restore as far as possible what was lost in the first place. This process of rebalancing ourselves offers the only real possibility of healing our spine.

This book will help the reader in discovering and unfolding their full potential.

In the first part we will learn how our spine is constructed and what tasks it is assigned to do. Later we will explore a number of pathological degenerations of our spine, with the aim of understanding how the symptoms of back pain come into being. The following chapters will help us to understand how the emotional and mental patterns manifest as spine problems. The second part provides support to those who are willing to learn how to help themselves to eliminate back problems completely. You will acquire powerful skills for the kinaesthetic awareness of life energy through movement, and a visual perception of it. The exercises described in the second part of the book are designed to rebalance your spine as far as possible. There are exercises for the lumbar spine, the thorax, and the neck and shoulder areas and for the whole spine. Practicing these exercises will cure your problems quickly and efficiently and above all it can prevent back pain from recurring again. In the third part of the book there are explanations on how to support others using safe, highly efficient, easy to learn healing techniques. Once you have reached this stage you may share your newly acquired skills with your loved ones to help them to relieve their pain and suffering. You will also learn the art of hands on healing and use techniques which have been specially developed to treat back pain in the lumbar area, the thorax, the neck and shoulder areas.

By doing this you will revive a hidden part of yourself. Such a discovery will not only cure your disorder but it will enrich your whole life.

PART ONE

Back Pain

CHAPTER 1

Physical Causes

The Blueprint of our Spine

The spine is the main axis of our whole body, and if we view our body as a temple, the spine is a place where divine principles manifest themselves as functions.

We can understand the special meaning of that axis for the whole construction if we learn how it comes into being in the very beginning. Our body grows out of one single cell where the unification of two poles – the female and the male – leads to the creation of a new individual. When a sperm penetrates an egg cell the fusion of these two initiates the evolution of a living being. A new cycle of life begins. When unified these two poles correspond exactly to the meaning of the Latin word *"deus"*, which means two or twins. This is the condition of a fertilized egg cell in the tube. To start a new cycle of creation, the unified poles need to separate again what was first manifested through a cell division. But the two cells now carry a bi-polar core within them and hence have the ability to continue to divide again. This goes on until the embryo is a cluster of between 40 and 150 cells with a central, fluid filled cavity in its centre, which is the very first stage in the evolution of our vertebral column. At this point the embryo is six days old and ready to be implanted in the mother's womb. What begins as the first division of cells continues in the separation into an inner layer which will grow into the embryonic body at a further stage, and an outer layer which will grow together with the womb and later build up the placenta.

The next expansion on the life's spiral is the division into three different germinal layers. Now this requires a much more specific adjustment of embryonic cells. Basically we speak about three germinal sheets which are linked together through a kind of tube.

Each of the three germinal sheets carries within themselves the potential to grow into some very highly specialized cells. With this the foundations are laid at the building site of our body's cathedral. Now the great variety of materials needed will be delivered. The stones needed to erect the walls, the timber for the construction of the roof, the marble to line the floors, and so on and so forth. Each single material serves a specific function within the entirety of the building. As these specialised cells begin to develop further they become interconnected. This interconnection literally becomes matter as our spine. The three germinal sheets are arranged in layers. The inner layer is called endoderm, the middle is mesoderm and the outer one is called ectoderm. These words have their origin in ancient Greek and literally mean inner layer, middle layer and outer layer. From the beginning they are connected through the neural tube which is the origin of the spinal cord and the brain. With further development of the neuronal tube, our embryo grows into the evolutionary stage of an amphibian which makes him look like a tadpole. Through this process we can observe how the embryo first develops a reptilian form, then the form of a fish where it breathes through the gills. Later our embryo will develop lungs and grow into a higher life form. Most of vertebrate's ancestors, fish as well as some reptiles, have no extremities so they can only move their bodies by winding. For this reason they have to be able to move in a sinuous curve. If there were only a uniform muscle on the right and the left side of an elastic stick it would be the same as a bow and an impulse for a forward movement could not be given. The muscle has to be sub-divided so that a graded movement is possible. It is the segmental harmonically coordinated contraction of muscles one behind the other which makes a snake glide. This segmentation along the spine creates areas innervated from one spinal nerve. Each of these spinal nerves consists of three branches, one for each germinal sheet. The role of the spinal nerve as a sensory branch for the ectoderm is to provide nerves for the skin, which is a kinaesthetic sensual organ. The nerve branching to the mesoderm provides the motor function of all skeletal muscles, which is necessary for any movement that we do intentionally. The vegetative branch for the endoderm is responsible for non-voluntary autonomic movement, like the heartbeat or the contraction of the intestinal muscles. Knowledge of this neural connection of organs, muscles and skin areas in a specific segment, provides the means to diagnose organic dysfunctions, as diseased organs often cause symptoms such as muscular tension in the assigned segmental area which is then experienced as back pain.

Let us move along the spiral of life once more with the aim of understanding what our spine really represents and how it is the main axis of the temple. On top of the spine we find the brain, our body's central steering unit. The neuronal cells which form our brain have their origins in the outer germinal layer, the ectoderm. This also forms the spinal cord. The motor neurons which are also neuronal cells are also connected directly to the vertebral column. Nothing can physically penetrate the brain. There is no light, no sound. Only electrochemical energy exists for the brain / mind. Everything physical, heat, light, sound, has to be translated into what we will later perceive with our brain mind. Only the body mind knows the physical world, the brain mind knows only symbols. These symbols are the language which translates the information from the body mind to the brain mind. The body mind experiences life directly and communicates with the brain mind by electrochemical transfer of neurons. The brain mind perceives life only from what has been initiated by the body mind. The communication between these two is one of the main functions of our spine. It is the medium which transfers the information from the body mind straight to the brain mind, except when the transfer of neuronal impulse goes straight from the receptor to the brain; this is the case with the senses received by the ears, nose, tongue and eyes. The actions we take as a reaction to these perceptions are a result of commands transmitted from our brain straight through the spine into the executing organs.

Tracing back to the tiniest detail of each bodily function, we will find that our vertebral column is the initial point for diversification into three different functions. One way to illustrate this is when you see an apple, you take it, eat it and digest it. This process is the transmission of information, movement and transformation all coordinated through the spine as the intermediary between our brain mind and our body mind.

Seen from the perspective of the spine, the mesoderm delivers the origin of those cell structures which later build up the bones of the vertebra. The cartilage, tendons, and the muscles which tie them up, are also part of the mesoderm. As a skeletal structure the spinal column is the central point for the head, the arms and the legs. It carries the weight of our body from the upper parts down to the pelvis and the feet. It holds the muscles of the neck and the extremities intact. But the spine is not an inflexible rod, it is amazingly flexible, especially when we bend to the front, the side, or extend to the back, or when we rotate around on our own axis. Like the shock absorber of a car, it reduces the impact when we walk or run and protects our very delicate brain.

The spinal column consists of 33-34 vertebra and intervertebral discs. Of these, there are the cervical spinal column which consists of seven vertebra, the thoracic which consists of twelve vertebra; the lumbar which consists of five vertebra, and finally the sacrum and coccyx. Adults have the five vertebra of the sacrum melted together, like the four to five vertebra of the coccyx. Seen from the side, the spine has the shape of an S. The convex curvatures to the front of the cervical and the lumbar spinal column are called lordosis. The convex curvatures to the back of the thoracic spinal column, the sacrum and the coccyx, are called kyphosis. At the end of the lumbar column the sacrum snaps sharply to the back and makes the end of the fifth lumbar vertebra rise out into the pelvis entrance. This so-called promon-

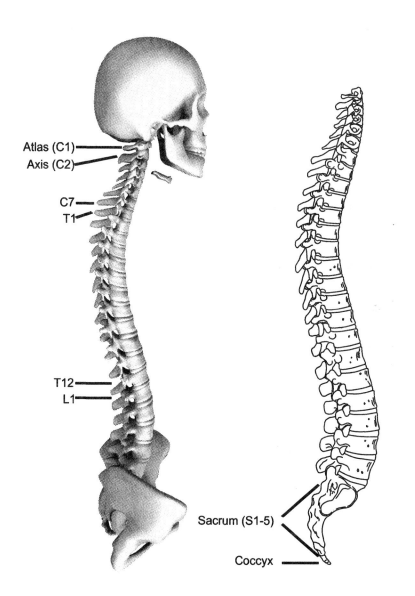

Atlas (C1)
Axis (C2)
C7
T1
T12
L1
Sacrum (S1-5)
Coccyx

torium shifts the emphasis of head and torso over the longitu-
dinal axis of the legs and gives humans the ability to walk
upright.

Each vertebra is made of a corpus and an arc. The corpuses of
the vertebra are connected by inter-vertebral discs. Their arcs are

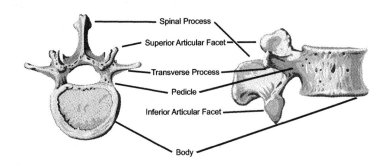

Spinal Process
Superior Articular Facet
Transverse Process
Pedicle
Inferior Articular Facet
Body

connected by small joints and also by a number of ligaments. Along the back of the vertebra and the corpuses, runs the spinal cord which is well protected by the vertebral channel. The spinal cord carries the motor and sensory nerve pathways to the trunk and legs, including the nerves that control bowel, bladder and sexual functions. The channel it runs through is limited backwards by vertebral arcs made from bone. The spinal nerves leave the vertebra channel through the foramina inter-vertebral, a kind of holes situated in between two such vertebral arcs.

The inter-vertebral discs consist of an outer layer made of strong collagen fibers and a gelatinous core which works like a shock absorber. These two layers build up a flexible connection between the vertebral corpuses, giving us the possibility to rotate and bend on the one hand, and providing a strong, firm hold between all the vertebral corpuses. It works as a shock absorber when the load changes from pressure into a pulling motion. Each disc is built like a sandwich which has two layers of hyaline cartilage and in between this is a gelatinous core, enclosed by a layer of strong collagen fibers. Due to the high osmotic concentration, the gelatinous core attracts water from its surroundings and causes swelling. Only when we are lying down or under water are these discs no longer under any stress or pressure. The swelling lengthens our vertebral column by about two centimetres. The collagen fibers around the core come under tension as soon as the "sandwich" is squeezed and the gelatinous core tries to move out of the way. The collagen fibers then begin to stretch and arch over the edge of the vertebral corpus.

Muscles and Movement

When we talk about back pain in general we should be aware of the fact that pain nerve endings located in various ligaments and muscles are mainly responsible for the discomfort we experience. If there is pain when someone is bending or rotating their trunk or head, the affected ligaments and muscles are no longer as flexible as they should be. Ligaments have the task of interconnecting the vertebra so that the spine is both stable and flexible. The ligaments of the spine are lined up in various directions. One runs over the whole length of the spine's front, connecting all the vertebral corpuses to each other. Another one covers the vertebral channel which the spinal cord runs through. These ligaments grow together with the upper and lower edge of the vertebral corpuses as well as with inter-vertebral discs, and they end at the lower lumbar spinal column. The arcs of the vertebra are connected by ligaments made of very elastic fibers which keep their high tension even in a normal position. To give the spine more stability there are also ligaments running crosswise between the vertebra.

Another type of ligament connects the lower and the upper edges of the vertebra. Directly from there a connection to the inter-spinal muscles begins. The deepest layer of muscles connected to the spine is the autochthonic back muscles. Some of them run straight along the whole spine, others run crosswise between the arcs of the vertebras.

These muscles are established at a very early embryonic stage and their innervations come directly from the back part of the spinal column, as opposed to all the other skeletal muscles which are innervated from the frontal part of the motor function branch of the spinal nerve.

This fact draws our attention because it is here that we find a directly connecting link between emotional states as well as mental patterns and our spine. Emotions and subconscious mental patterns will both manifest in a special type of body posture. Emotions and thoughts pass straight from the brain to the spine and directly affect the autochthon back muscles, where the patterns occur as altered tension in the related segments. Here they cause a number of destructive processes which will end up in such heavy degeneration of tissue that a prolapsed disc, for example, will be the result. How this happens is discussed in detail later in this book. It is enough for now to know that this type of muscles is where we find the origin of most complaints related to back pain. Like all skeletal muscles the autochthon back muscles consist of bundles of fibers, or muscle cells. These muscle cells consist of a bundle of strings called fibrils which are responsible for the muscles' contraction. Each of these muscle cells or muscle fibers is completely covered by a skin of connective tissue, and each bundle of fibers also has a skin, as does the entire muscle itself. The skin interconnects the single parts within the muscle and is responsible for the return to its original state after contracting or stretching. If a muscle is working properly a stimulus from the motor function branch of the spinal nerve initiates a very complex chemical reaction which ends up in the contraction of single fibrils which then leads to the contraction of a whole muscle. Each muscle is fixed by ligaments to bones of an extremity (such as a hand, a finger or a toe), or in the case of the autochthon back muscles directly to a vertebra.

A movement begins when a muscle contracts. For example, when the quadriceps – the big muscle on the front of your upper leg – contracts, the whole leg is then lifted up. To achieve the full range of this movement the muscles on the back of the leg and the bottom have to stretch, these are the so-called antagonists here. On the much smaller areas between single vertebra we find the same mechanism working within the autochthon back muscles.

Sometimes a muscle is unable to relax again after contracting. This occurs because of a constant overburdening of particular skeletal muscles over a period of time. The reason could be due to destructive body movements and postures such as sitting for many hours at the computer or lifting patients from their beds as nurses used to do. Destructive internal stimuli such as negative emotional states, or external ones like hypothermia and draughts, can also bring muscle cells into a state of permanent contraction. The background on how this works on an emotional level will be explained further on.

Whether there is an internal or an external stimuli or a mechanical overburdening, the result is a permanent contraction of the muscle. Even if only one amongst the thousands of fibrils within a muscle contracts without relaxing, a vicious cycle begins. Starting with one fibril the whole muscle's metabolism begins to change. First it happens only in one single muscle cell, later in a whole bundle of them. At this point a reduction of flexibility and pain of a different kind is experienced by an individual affected by such a problem. A great number of autochthon back muscles are very small. It is possible for a complete muscle to fall into a state of pathogen tension. In this case, a muscle will have changed from an aerobic to an anaerobic metabolism. What this means is that no oxygen is reaching the muscle cells and lactic acid accumulates as a decomposition product within the tissue. Now the muscle builds up a state of high tension so that no more blood can get in to the tissue, which makes it impossible to remove all the lactic acid. Enclosed within the muscle are a number of nerve endings which become compressed at this stage. As soon as the muscle is stretched, as an antagonist through the contraction of its protagonist, intense pain is felt. To avoid pain the body tries to avoid movement in the affected segment and even more tension builds up in all the muscles which are connected to those which were showing symptoms at first.

To get a picture of such a process and its consequences for an individual, think of a man, around 40 years of age, whom we will call Stan. Stan usually does not move a lot. He is not exactly sporty. He is a little overweight, not only from a sedentary lifestyle and lack of movement, but also because he loves to eat a lot of meat, sugar and white flour, a diet which keeps his body in a permanent state of hyperacidity. After being pressured by his wife, Stan gives in and decides to mow the lawn. He goes to the garage to get his lawn mower. The handle grip is set too low for him so he has to bend his back all the time while working with it. He sweats a lot because he is working hard. Stan doesn't realize that he is overstretching all the tiny muscles running crosswise between the arcs of his third and fourth lumbar vertebra. This is because Stan has very weak stomach muscles, so all the weight of his trunk rests mainly on the autochthon muscles and the ligaments of his spine. A soft breeze eases Stan's profuse perspiration, but this pleasure does not last long. Only a few minutes and this cooling will end in a disaster. Just one single fibril in one of those overburdened tiny muscles reacts to this stimulus by permanently contracting. Stan continues to enjoy the breeze on his back without taking any notice of the dramatic changes within his autochthon muscles. Clusters of connected muscle cells continuously build up until the whole muscle has reached a grade of tension so that hardly any blood reaches it to nourish the cells and supply them with new oxygen. As soon as Stan straightens his torso he immediately feels a terrible pain in his back and is unable to get up. This happens because all the nerve endings within the contracted muscle have been squeezed and the over-contracted muscle has no more flexibility. With lightning speed an additional number of connected muscles have contracted until they were also in permanent tension. Now the poor man is unable to move. Limping and complaining Stan leaves his garden in search of help. All he wants now is to get rid of his problem, and this problem has a name – lumbago.

Such primary muscular tension can also create a lot of

additional collateral damage. If a nerve root is set under pressure by a blocked vertebral segment, it results in pain being emitted into the extremities. This can occur in the legs when a segment located somewhere at the lumbar vertebra is affected. The lumbago which affected Stan seems to him to have come out of the blue, whereas the tension in the neck and shoulder areas are usually felt as discomfort over a long period before they manifest as serious problems. Lisa works in a call centre. She has to talk to customers and use the computer to get the information the customer needs. She sits day in day out for countless hours at her desk, wearing her headset, eyes fixed on the screen, her fingers moving over the keyboard. While sitting there she is looking down all the time. This not only stresses the autochthon muscles in her neck permanently but also the bigger muscles situated closer to the surface, such as the muscle which turns our head from side to side, or the trapezius, which covers the whole back of the chest up to the neck. These are in a state of permanent tension because of this continuous head down posture. In addition, a lot of tension builds up in a group of smaller muscles which are fixed on either sides of the shoulder blades and the thoracic vertebra. A number of other muscles along the neck and shoulder are affected too. Their natural range of movement is restricted by this continuous habitual posture of sitting at the computer. The stress which is always present in such a job like Lisa's aggravates the ongoing destructive process. The lack of movement leads to a poor blood supply to the whole neck and shoulder area and in combination with a poor diet consisting basically of coffee, sweets, fizzy canned drinks and fast food snacks like industrial prepackaged sandwiches, would lead to a serious hyperacidicity in her muscle cells.

In the end, the lack of blood circulation will slowly change the area into a kind of a living dump. Clearly this will not support any further development of the ligaments, joints and bone structures like the vertebral joints or discs within the affected area. An inclination to inflammation and further degeneration of tissue will be the result. At first Lisa will only feel tired and uncomfortable, later there will be some pain from time to time but it will not last long enough for her to start to thinking about making lifestyle changes. The next stage will be serious back pain, permanent restrictions in her head movements and pain emitting into her arms, at times accompanied by a severe frontal headache. It is at this stage that she recognises she really needs some kind of physiotherapy.

What can be done in such a case? Basically there are two main ways to help the affected muscles recover efficiently. Firstly you have to ensure that the blood circulation is increased to change the metabolism back to a physiologically normal state. Hot packs made from fango – which is a kind of clay – or from moor, are recommended. They heat up the skin covering the affected muscles and widen the capillaries allowing more blood to flow through. The local application of ultrasound is very useful because it has a better impact on the deeper layers of the muscles.

To support such a process and make it much more efficient, remedial massage performed by a well trained therapist is highly recommended. It will mechanically crack up all the clusters of contracted bundles of muscle cells called myogelosis. This is done with the aim of mobilising the whole muscle so that it can rebalance between muscle cell contraction and relaxation again. Recovering the flexibility and getting an access to the full range of movement is the second requirement for a successful therapy.

The disadvantage of such a treatment is that deeper layers of autochthon muscles often cannot be reached so they do not benefit. Unfortunately in most cases this the key and the root cause for further deterioration. So if they are not reached during therapy the symptoms will show up again soon. Chiropractors have a much deeper impact here and are often successful in breaking segmental blockages within the autochthon muscles. However this kind of treatment contains considerable risk for the patient as the manipulation is done with a lot of force and may cause serious damage to nerve roots or can even result in complete paralysis. Also, occasionally discs may rupture or there may be micro traumas on ligaments or little vertebral joints which will become inflamed.

Degenerative or Ageing Changes

Tissue degeneration is a natural result of ageing, a biochemical process where so-called free radicals play a decisive role. Free radicals come into being as a metabolism fall-out and in many cases they penetrate the body as a by-product of smoking or by accidental absorption of toxic substances from the environment. They are extremely destructive to the body's cells and are responsible for a number of severe degenerative diseases such as cancer. Free radicals are also extremely destructive to the cartilage cells and bony material of our spine. There are a number of reasons why tissue becomes vulnerable to such destructive influences. The first one is genetic predisposition; another is overburdening through over-use, and another is the permanent under-supply of vitamins and vital trace minerals vital for the metabolism. Besides poor diet, a lack of nourishment of the skeletal structure has its roots in inflexible and tensed muscles which have a poor metabolism. Bony and cartilage tissue covered by hyper acidic muscles will no longer be supplied with blood as they would be in a healthy body, so that metabolic waste is not removed and nutrients do not arrive in the required quantity.

If there are symptoms in the lumbar or in the neck and shoulder area, it is a good idea to see a doctor or medical practitioner in case a problem starts to cause permanent pain. Whatever therapy is followed, the first step is to find the physical origin of the pain. This is the safest way to avoid damage which can result from the wrong therapy. This also reduces the risk of severe diseases and organ dysfunctions being overlooked, which often tend to show themselves first as back pain and can develop into serious conditions if they are not discovered in time. Therapy of any kind based on presumptions rather than knowledge, will not be of advantage in many cases. It will be useless or – in the worst case scenario – even dangerous to the patient. Normally the doctor's diagnosis should include at least an X-ray but an MRI examination of the spine would be even better. An X-ray would show damage on osseous tissue, but in contrast an MRI has the ability to show softer tissues like cartilage ligaments, organs and nerves.

The results of such a check up will contain terms that most people have neither heard of nor have any idea of their meanings.

Spondylosis occurs as soon as one reaches the age of 40 and above. The term *spondylosis* is a whole process of tissue degeneration in which back pain often has its origin. *Spondylosis* starts with the gradual drying out of the nucleus portion of a disc. What this means is that the water content of the nucleus decreases with age and affects its shock absorbing quality. The degenerative effects of ageing may weaken the structure of the annulus portion of the disc and the vertebral bodies come to lie closer together. As a result of the height loss, facet joints will be distorted and this can cause wear and tear changes in them. Each vertebral body has four facet joints that work like hinges. These are the moving joints of the spine enabling extension (arching back), flexion (bending forward), and rotation. As disc material slowly wears out, ligaments loosen and excess motion occurs at the joint. The body naturally and necessarily thickens the ligaments that hold the bones together. Over time, the thick ligaments tend to calcify, resulting in flecks of bone or bone spur formation.

Additionally there are a number of problems related to the original drying out of the discs' nucleus. The narrowing of the disc space causes the annulus portion to bulge over the edges of the vertebra corpus. This does not usually cause symptoms but if the bulging is excessive, nerve roots may be compressed with resultant symptoms. Normally the bulge is centrally located and as there is usually plenty of room in the spinal canal, nerve roots are rarely compressed. But a lateral bulge, if very large, may sometimes compress a nerve root. In the situation where a cervical nerve root is severely irritated or compressed there will be a severe sharp pain radiating all the way down the arm and into the forearm, aggravated by neck movement, possibly with numbness and tingling in a portion of the hand, fingers or arm, and possibly also with weakness of arm or hand muscles supplied by that nerve. There may also be pain around the shoulder blades. A nerve root may be irritated or compressed by bulging of the part of the disc that lies in front of the nerve – the most lateral portion of the disc – not the central portion.

Ageing is often associated with the formation of a bony out growth at the periphery of the vertebral body. The medical term for bone spurs is *osteophytes*, and they represent an enlargement of the normal bony structure. They can grow in each direction, forward or backward. As long as we can find them only on the front or at the side they will not cause any problems. But when they occur backwards this occasionally can cause a narrowing of the spinal canal. If very severe spinal canal narrowing occurs, the spinal cord may be compressed, causing neurological symptoms. Some individuals are born with an unusually narrow spinal canal which predisposes them to spinal cord compression as the normal ageing changes progresses. This condition called *spinal stenosis* can cause nerve pinching, leading to pain down the legs that becomes worse when the patient stands or walks and is better when seated. The incidence of these ageing changes is affected by heredity. Some families are predisposed to develop marked changes at an early age.

Spondylolisthesis is another mysterious term and means the slipping forward of an upper vertebra on the lower one. This can happen to children when the place where the corpus joins the arc is made of gristle instead of bone. While the gristle is very strong, it is not as strong as bone. Over time it may stretch, permitting the

upper vertebra to slip forward onto the lower one. In the older population, degenerative disc disease, *spondylosis*, usually leads to "slipping vertebras" – *spondylolisthesis*. This occurs most commonly in the fourth and fifth lumbar vertebrae. Lumbar degenerative disc disease usually starts with a torsional (twisting) injury to the lower back, such as when a person rotates to put something on a shelf or swing a golf club. However, the pain is also frequently caused by simple wear and tear on the spine.
• "Slipping vertebras" is common in ballet dancers and acrobats who arch their backs a lot. The majority of people with it have no symptoms. But symptoms (backache) can occur in a person with pre-existing and painless *spondylolisthesis* as the result of a strain or lifting. Once symptoms start, they tend to recur. In *spondylolisthesis*, pain is usually confined to the back, although nerve root irritation caused by the instability of the adjacent bones may cause leg pain similar to that caused by a herniated disc. The pain is characteristically intermittent and is brought on by activity.

Spinal arthritis or *osteoarthritis of the facet joints* is often referred to ageing changes. This condition is a common cause of back pain in the older middle-aged patient population (those over 55 or 60) caused by wearing of the cartilage that covers and acts as a cushion inside joints, in providing a self-lubricating low-friction gliding surface. The condition of facet arthritis can cause stiffness and lower back pain that is usually worse in the morning, gets better after moving around, then gets worse again at the end of the day. The most common root cause of cervical and lumbar arthritis is repetitive trauma to the spine from recreational or work related excessive strains. Patients may typically develop symptoms of *osteoarthritis* in their mid-forties to early fifties. Men are more likely to develop arthritic related symptoms earlier in life, however postmenopausal women with stiffening spines (accelerated bone spur formation) rapidly approach men in incidence and severity of *osteoarthritis*.

◢Herniated disc is probably the most common degenerative

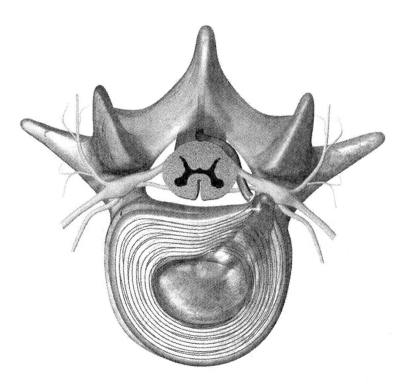

change; disc herniation is known to nearly everybody. Suffering a herniated disk one may have a difficult time with ordinary movements, including sitting or bending over. There are sharp pains in the back or down one of the legs. In severe cases one may have difficulty with even simple movements, preferring to lie down in one position for hours at a time. Pain can be so intense that one may feel that it is harming the body to allow it to continue. But herniated disks are not likely to result in paralysis except in rare instances. The disc is made of a tough outer layer called the *annulus fibrosus* and a gel-like centre called the *nucleus pulposus*. As one gets older, the centre of the disc may start to lose water content, making the disc less effective as a cushion. As a disc deteriorates, the outer layer can also tear. This can allow displacement of the disc's centre (called a herniated or ruptured disc) through a crack in the outer layer, into the space occupied by the nerves and spinal cord. In the case of herniated cervical disc it presses on the nerves and cause pain, numbness, tingling or weakness in the shoulders or arms. In most cases disc herniation will occur between the fourth and the fifth lumbar vertebra or between the fifth lumbar vertebra and the sacrum. Nerve impingement from a herniated disc between the fourth and the fifth lumbar vertebra can cause weakness in extension of the big toe and potentially in the ankle (foot drop). Numbness and pain can be felt on the top of the foot, and the pain may also radiate into the back. Nerve impingement from a herniated disc between the fifth lumbar vertebra and the sacrum may cause loss of the ankle reflex and weakness in ankle push off (so that the person cannot do toe rises). Numbness and pain can radiate down to the sole or the outside of the foot.

Bechterew's disease is an inflammatory arthritis that affects the spinal column, sacroiliac joints and sometimes the hips. It occurs almost exclusively in young males. It produces fusion of the spinal column, sometimes in a flexed position so that victims of it have trouble seeing where they are going. It is characterised by intermittent flare ups of back pain often with leg radiation so that it can mimic a herniated disc. Eventually the process burns out, leaving the patient with a stiff but painless spine. Its cause is unknown. Although some authorities believe that trauma plays a role in its onset, the evidence is that it is not caused by trauma. ✦

Schuermann's disease is an abnormality of the growth plates that are on the upper and lower surfaces of the vertebral body before skeletal maturation. It can result in a marked increase in the normal rounding (kyphosis) of the thoracic spine in adolescents. It is seldom a cause of back pain: its principle effect is cosmetic.

⁊The *sacroiliac joints* are located at the bottom of the back. You have one on either side of the spine. The sacroiliac joints help make up the rear part of the pelvic girdle and sit between the sacrum and the ilia. There are torsional or twisting forces applied to the pelvic girdle when the lower limbs are moved. These limbs act like long levers and without the sacroiliac joints and the pubic symphysis (at the front of the pelvis) which allows movement, the pelvis would very likely be subject to a fracture. These joints can often get stuck or in some cases one half of the pelvis can glide forwards or backwards, which is often referred to as a twisted pelvis. When this occurs it often irritates the iliolumbar ligament which results in inflammation. This is usually indicated by tenderness around the bony lumps which you can feel if you place your thumbs on either side of your lower back. Inflammation of the sacroiliac joints and associated ligaments is very common, especially following pregnancy where hormones are released and this result in the relaxation of ligaments in preparation for childbirth. In most cases the causes of sacroiliitis are mechanical.

Symptoms occurring from problems related to the *sacroiliac joints* include pain located either to the left or right of your lower back. The pain can range from an ache to a sharp pain which can restrict movement. The pain may radiate out into your buttocks and lower back and will often radiate round to the front into the groin. Occasionally it is responsible for pain in the testicles among males. There may be referred pain into the lower limb which can be mistaken for sciatica. Classic symptoms are difficulty in turning over in bed, struggling to put on shoes and socks and pain in getting your legs in and out of the car. Stiffness appears in the lower back when getting up after sitting for long periods and when getting up from bed in the morning. Occasionally an aching occurs to one side of your lower back when driving long distances. •

Scoliosis is sideways curvature of the spine. As the curve increases, the ribs on the concave side are jammed together forcing the vertebrae to rotate. In turn this makes the ribs on the convex side more prominent causing a "hump back". Any type of scoliosis is often associated with premature ageing changes in the discs at the apex of the curve. It can cause back pain. But in a recent survey of patients who had films of the abdomen made (usually looking for kidney stones) a considerable proportion had scoliosis with ageing change but had no back pain symptoms. Thus in patients who have scoliosis and claim work related back symptoms, the facts must be interpreted with caution.

Sciatic scoliosis is sometimes seen in acute disc protrusions. It is not a structural deformity of the back but the result of muscle spasm.

To recapitulate, most degenerative or ageing changes result in a state of back pain which can occur occasionally but in many cases tends to end up in permanent pain. The more an individual's discs, cartilage and bony structures of the vertebra and their interconnecting joints are damaged, the greater the tendency of the ligaments and muscles to be inflamed or to increase in tension. We know that a lot of nerve endings are located here so it is easy to understand that permanent irritation of these may cause back pain occasionally or even permanently. Such permanent pain is sometimes experienced as subliminal but it can also be acute. Both are torturous and restrictive and take away a lot of quality of life from an affected individual. This is also true with the *sacroiliac joints* as problems there do not have their origin directly in tissue degeneration. But heavy disc degeneration may be the reason for a change within the structural construction of the whole spine and at one point this will in all probability cause problems and related symptoms in the *sacroiliac joints* as well.

Unfortunately it is not possible to restore tissue once it is destroyed. But it is possible to avoid further degeneration. This goes hand in hand with a recovery of ligaments and muscles through a systemic re-education of body structures so that they learn to compensate for the degenerations and resulting symptoms. But this works only when we learn to develop a holistic approach to include not only the physical but also the emotional, mental and spiritual aspect of a body as a whole. What is very important here is a phenomenon called *chi* or *life energy* which has to do a lot with the whole process of tissue ageing. But this will be discussed later, for now we will focus on some other physical reasons which lead directly to back pain.

Severe Diseases and Organ Dysfunction

Back pain is often seen as a side effect of severe diseases including *osteoporosis, cancer,* and inflammation of the bony part of the spine. But even when such illnesses become incurable or the sufferer is close to a terminally ill state, it is still possible to ease their pain. This requires not only accurate medication but also someone who has the skills to support the patient effectively. But although there is a chance to improve an individual's situation, the opportunities for this are not limitless. It is essential to remember that with degenerative changes it is not possible to restore tissue once it has been destroyed. All one can do is to activate the human body to cope with the situation as well as possible. How this works and why will be demonstrated later when we discuss the phenomenon of life energy in detail.

By possessing appropriate knowledge, sufferers may be able to help themselves to some extent. In the case of *osteoporosis* there is a real chance to improve things, particularly if the progress of the disease has not gone too far. Once pain is relieved the affected person can do a lot for themselves in terms of slowing down the onslaught of the diseases. Advanced states of *osteoporosis* appear mainly in older people and they are the ones who really need a helping hand first. *Osteoporosis* is a disease in which bones become fragile and are more likely to break – hence it is known as brittle bone disease. These broken bones, or fractures, occur typically in the hip, spine, and wrist. Any bone can be affected, but of special concern are fractures of the hip and spine. Spinal or vertebral fractures have serious consequences, including loss of height, severe back pain, and deformity. *Osteoporosis* is also a bone disease in which the bone mineral density is reduced, bone micro architecture is disrupted, and the amount and variety of non-collagenous proteins in bone is altered. The underlying mechanism in all cases of *osteoporosis* is an imbalance between wearing down of bone and bone formation. Either bone tear down is excessive, or bone formation is diminished, or in some cases, both. The mechanisms influencing the formation of the disease are complex and in most cases it is not simply as a result of inadequate calcium intake. Low peak bone mass is the contributory factor in the development of *osteoporosis*. Bone mass peaks in both men and women between the ages of 25 and 35, and after that it begins to diminish. Achieving a higher peak bone mass through exercise and proper nutrition during adolescence is highly important for the prevention of *osteoporosis*. Due to its hormonal component, more women suffer from *osteoporosis* than men, particularly after menopause. The possibility of bone remodelling is heavily influenced by nutritional and hormonal factors, calcium and vitamin D are nutrients required for normal bone growth. Different hormones regulate the mineral composition of bone, with higher levels causing the slow break down of calcium and bone. Oestrogens and testosterone increase bone growth, the loss of oestrogens following menopause causes a phase of rapid bone loss. Similarly, testosterone levels in men diminish with advancing age and are related to male *osteoporosis*. In addition, *osteoporosis* may be caused by various hormonal conditions, such as smoking and medications. The risk increases when you lead a sedentary lifestyle with little or no weight bearing exercise, or walking; having a family history of *osteoporosis*, and being over 30 years of age. Men and women in that age group are at equal risk.

Physical activity helps bone remodelling. People who remain physically active throughout their life have a lower risk of osteoporosis. Conversely, people who are bedridden are at a significantly increased risk. Physical activity has its greatest impact during adolescence, affecting peak bone mass most. In adults, physical activity helps maintain bone mass, and can increase it by 1% or 2%. Exercise is of great importance for people suffering from *osteoporosis*. Regular load bearing exercises can help to delay the onset of the condition and can also help to relieve pain. This is because regular movement can help to keep joints supple. Sufferers of *osteoporosis* must learn to judge their own pain thresholds and exercise accordingly. However, excessive exercise can lead to damage to the bone structures. There are all too many examples of marathon runners who have developed severe *osteoporosis* later in life. In the absence of treatment, overt *osteoporosis* is triggered by a fracture. Some fractures, such as vertebral compression fractures or sacral insufficiency fractures, may not be apparent at first, either symptom-less or appearing to patient and physician as a very bad back ache. An estimated 700,000 women have a first vertebral fracture each year. The lifetime risk of a clinically detected symptomatic vertebral fracture is about 15% in a 50-year-old white woman. However, because symptoms are often overlooked or thought to be a normal part of ageing, it is believed that only about one-third of vertebral compression fractures are actually diagnosed.

Within the spine *tuberculosis* or *osteomyelitis* or *discitis* can occasionally occur and each of these three infectious inflammatory conditions causes back pain. *Bone tuberculosis* affects the small bones within hands and feet and mostly the vertebra of the lower thoracic and the upper lumbar spine. Often a number of joining vertebras are afflicted; the infection there leads to the destruction of the whole vertebra including the discs. Other infectious inflammations of bones are called *osteomyelitis*, but they seldom occur within the spine. *Discitis* is a bacterial or viral infection of discs which affects mainly children up to the age of ten. The infection leads to severe back pain which increases through movement of the spine. The pain occurs mainly in the lower back and the thoracic area, from there the pain emits into other parts of the body, the stomach, the hips and the legs.

Cancer as well as a number of other severe inner organ diseases causes back pain affecting the spine indirectly. This is a very important point to remember when back pain occurs. Spinal tumours can be either benign or malignant. Malignant tumours growing from bones are rare. They are usually metastasis beginning from the breast, the lungs, the prostate, kidneys, liver or thyroid. In cases where tumours grow out of vertebra they will cause a number of spine related problems and pain within the back because a change of bone structure occasionally ends up in damaged discs and facet joints or/and in compressed nerve roots.

Often people who suffer from severe back pain and do not find an obvious reason for this within all skeletal structures have to look for some other explanations. One possibility here can be that physical pain may have an emotional origin. This is discussed in the next chapter.

Another reason for such an inexplicable occurrence of pain can be found in some special characteristics spinal nerves possess. Corresponding to each germinal sheet of the embryonic evolution the spinal nerves support a number of different specific functions when they leave the spinal cord. Spinal nerves consist of three different branches. A sensual one called *dermatome*, which interconnects the skin and the sensual organs to the spinal cord and the brain. Another branch is called *myotom* and supports the motoric movement of the skeletal muscles. The third one is called *enterotom* and is a separate branch which includes the symphaticus and parasymphaticus nerve. This branch is responsible for the inner organs. And in cases when such an organ shows severe dysfunction the skin and the muscles react as well. This is because of the interconnection between the three branches of the spinal nerve.

When somebody suffers from *gastritis* without showing any obvious symptoms, and the dysfunction stays in a sub-acute state within the system, the muscles and sometimes the skin may show typical signs. It depends on the segment supported by the spinal nerve which is responsible for the specific organ where such side effects will occur. In case of the stomach this will be between the fifth and the ninth thoracic vertebra on the left side of the body.

The affected individual may first recognise problems such as increased muscular tension between the third and fourth cervical vertebras. This will be felt not only in the stomach but also in a number of other affected organs. To find out which is the affected one it is necessary to examine the area between the fifth and the ninth thoracic vertebra, as in the case of the stomach. If we find increased muscular tension, the suspicion of *gastritis* is confirmed. This is true for every other organ. We should also be aware that organs situated on the right side of the body show more signs there, and those on the left side of the body will show signs in this part. Some organs which are in pairs, like the kidneys or the lungs, will show signs on both sides of the body. In cases where one finds out that something is wrong within an organ it is best to see the doctor as soon as possible. The overview below will give an idea of where organic related signs of dysfunction occur on the back.

Both Sides
Lungs   Th3-Th10
Small Intestine   Th8-Th11
Large Intestine   Th9-L1
Kidneys and Bladder   Th9-Th12, L1-L2
Gonads   Th10-L1
Right Side
Duodenum   Th6-Th10
Liver, Gall Bladder   Th6-Th10
Left Side
Heard   Th1-Th8
Stomach   Th5-Th9
Spleen, Pancreas   Th7-Th10

CHAPTER 2

Emotional Influence

What is an Emotion

Emotions set us in motion. Seen from this angle there is a connection between emotions which move us on a psychological level and skeletal muscles which move us on a physical level. Once we recognise the mutual influence and interaction taking place between emotions and muscles, we are able to see that different patterns of movements create body postures which lead directly to spine problems. In analyzing how our emotional life manifests itself within our musculoskeletal system, it is helpful to consider the Western and the Eastern approaches to health and healing, so as to reap the benefits of both viewpoints. First let's focus on the Western concept of what emotions mean. Feelings are separate from emotions because a feeling does not essentially include a cognitive aspect. This basically means that it is not necessary to understand what happens in your body when you feel pain, unlike emotions which contain a value judgement like right or wrong or good and bad. Moods and feelings are different from emotions and uncontrollable reactions. Moods and more fleeting feelings both possess the ability to influence perception in a way that reality is seen from a state of mind such as "I'm happy" or "I'm sad". What emotions, feelings and moods have in common is the distinction of being experienced as being enjoyable or not. For example, there is no bad mood without the presence of displeasure.

Aristotle (384BC-322 BC) understood emotions as a psychic experience with the fundamental attributes of being pleasant or unpleasant. This point of view continued until the beginning of the 20th century and was supported by the German psychologist *Hermann Ebbinghaus* (1850-1909). Contrary to this, his colleague

Philip Lersch (1898-1972) argued against what he postulated: "The understanding of emotions will be trivialized if we try to compare the experience of being touched by a piece of art to the feelings we experience when we enjoy a glass of good wine. It does not seem to be appropriate to put a feeling like remorse on the same level as any other trivial feelings of discomfort. But when we look at religious feelings or those of respect or devotion it seems virtually impossible to categorise them either as being pleasant or as unpleasant."

Wilhelm Wundt (1832-1920), a German philosopher who first established psychology as an independent scientific branch, expanded the view of ancient Greeks. In addition to the basic principle of pleasant/unpleasant experiences he included concepts such as tension/ release and excitement and tranquillity. The American psychologist *William James* (1842-1910) postulated that emotions are not perceivable without intense physical reactions. According to James, our emotional experience is largely due to the experience of bodily changes. If we were to follow his idea it would mean that we do not flee from the bear because we are frightened of it but rather fear is felt because of the bodily changes that take place when we run away from the bear. The Portuguese brain researcher *Antonio Damasio* supports this view: "In my opinion the nature of emotion is found within all the countless changes of physical stages which are activitated in all the different organs through nerve endings."

According to the *Two Factor Theory of Emotion* of *Schachter & Singer*, emotions arise as a result of physiological stimuli such as tachycardia and blushing. It depends on the situation how stimuli are interpreted. Palpitation of the heart is perceived as a strain when we do a workout, but when a young man flirts with a beautiful woman his increased heartbeat in response to her presence is a sensation experienced as an emotion. Many of us will have experienced the body's common response to *shame* as a sensation of warmth in the upper chest and face, the response to *fear* as a heightened heartbeat, 'flinch' response, and muscular tension. The sensations connected with *anger* are almost indistinguishable from fear. *Happiness* is often felt as an expansive or swelling feeling in the chest and the sensation of lightness or buoyancy, as if standing underwater. *Sadness* occurs as a feeling of tightness in the throat and eyes, with heaviness or relaxation in the arms and legs. *Desire* can be accompanied by a dry throat and heavy breathing. The intensity of any emotion is determined by the intensity of the physiological stimulus but the quality of emotion depends on the interpretation of the situation.

Another completely different understanding of emotions independent of the Western academic scientific point of view is worth mentioning here as well. Around 400-500 BC Aristotle's predecessors, the Phytagorean, the Eleates and others, greatly influenced his teachings and concepts. Around the same time in ancient China, philosophers postulated their understanding of emotions. Their teachings of *The Five Elements* are a way to describe how nature works as seen from a cosmological perspective, and how a number of cosmic principles manifest themselves as functions in perpetual repetition. The way these elements interact produces harmony or destructive chaos. This concept can be understood as an analogy to the Western *Four Elements* introduced by Aristotle's predecessors. According to *Empedocles* (490BC-430BC) the teaching of *Four Elements* looks at the fundamental components of material which underlines the static characteristics of everything that exists. In contrast, *Heraclites* (535BC-475BC) looks at the laws which underline the process of coming into being, to be and to die away as the dynamic changes within the living.

This coincides with the ancient Chinese concept of a human body made up of *Five Elements* or *states of chang*. Each one of these elements is the embodiment of a natural principle occurring on physical as well as emotional levels. These principles also manifest themselves as external stimuli in nature such as hot,

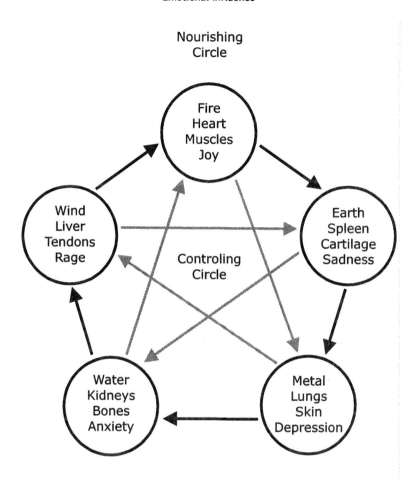

cold, or a climatic phenomenon such as wind. The *Five Elements* are each associated with a season, a direction, and they are often defined as a quality of taste, a sense organ, a sensual function, and each element is assigned to a pair of internal organs (situated towards the back and front of the body) and a type of tissue.

This idea is not exclusive to the Chinese. The Native Americans and the ancient Egyptians developed similar concepts. But the Chinese approach is the only complete system to have survived and it is still practised daily all over the world, in the form of traditional Chinese medicine, including acupuncture, acupressure massage, medical herbalism, and all related disciplines.

When we look at an emotional state from the Taoist angle, the typical functional characteristics can be associated with a specific emotional state attributed to one of the five elements or states of change. The result is a better understanding of the impact that an emotional state can have on such a complex system like the human being and how this affects our skeletal muscles as well as our spine.

We will now focus on the five emotional states according to the *Five Elements*. We will analyze their functions and look at what happens when an imbalance occurs as back pain, or worse, as the origin of degenerating changes within our spine.

Anxiety

Everyone experiences anxiety in some form. Anxiety is absolutely necessary for survival, for humans as well as animals. Maybe you think that anxiety is the dark side of a life full of pleasure. Maybe you think that anxiety is a disorder of the mind or an accident of creation which has to be eliminated. However, you have to accept that anxiety is an emotion.

According to *Sigmund Freud* (1856-1939) anxiety originates when there is a state of increased excitement which leads to congestion and is the biological background to the experience of anxiety. *Psychoanalysis* tells us that each state of panic grows out of the primary trauma of birth. This explains anxiety as a learned reaction in the sense of a classical conditioning. The philosopher *Martin Heidegger* (1889-1976) adds that the whole range of anxiety reaches from the cradle to the grave.

A new view on the nature of anxiety was confirmed by the experiments done by *Schachter & Singer*. Drugs increasing activity and drugs lessening activity were administered to subjects. During a period of waiting for the experiment to begin (an experiment which never really took place) the researchers staged accidental incidents on subjects with the aim of bringing them into a either a cheerful or an angry mood. What they tried to create was an emotional state within the subjects but what actually happened was something else. It turned out that without increased activity produced by pharmaceuticals as a trigger, no emotions were aroused at all. And when this happened the intensity of emotion depended on the level of activity created through medication. This result can be interpreted in the following way: that anxiety like any other emotion is an activity without specific content. This means anxiety is an abstract notion. Besides plain anxiety there is the concept of fear which is an innate reaction to awkward or life threatening situations. Plain anxiety is seen as the peak of psychic abstraction.

Anxiety exists within the deepest layer of our souls as a state of permanent tension which keeps us alert against everything and nothing. This is a basic requirement in order to enable us to survive in an environment of 'eat or be eaten'. Wherever you go, anxiety will be with you. It will always be with you as it is probably the most important requirement to get anywhere at all. Anxiety makes us cautious, sharpens our senses and improves our intellect. Our physical strengths are constantly on alert because of anxiety and that enables us to react either explosively or to endure seemingly endless situations. All in all anxiety is an essential manifestation of Life Energy.

The etymological meaning of anxiety is narrowing or tightness. This is easily comprehensible because when we are anxious we become tense and our throats narrow. Chinese Taoists, ancient Egyptians and Native Americans all say anxiety is a specific manifestation of Life energy on an emotional level. To trace the cosmic principle underlying anxiety we need to take a closer look at its main characteristic. What is anxiety doing? It is narrowing and increasing tension. These are typical contracting characteristics. When we apply this idea to our skeletal muscles, we discover that permanent anxiety creates a state of permanent contraction within our muscular system. This is an advantage as long as we benefit from an increased readiness to react to a dangerous situation. But when this condition is permanent or chronic it becomes destructive and will lead to a state of muscular torpor.

How does an emotion become the origin for serious spine problems? A constant state of anxiety is a common source of lower back problems. To tremble with anxiety is similar to trembling with cold. Both the feeling of anxiety and the sensation of cold cause contraction of the skeletal muscles. But there is a difference between feeling cold and anxiety. Feeling cold is a very strong and immediate stimulus whereas the physical effects of anxiety are a subtle build up over a longer period time. The result is a loss of flexibility which restricts our ability to move. Restriction of movement, which often goes unrecognised for a long time, interrupts the Life energy flow along the spine, resulting in the degeneration of intervertebral discs. This may ultimately cause a prolapsed disc, the origins of which had been hidden in an obvious emotional pattern.

When anxiety begins to build up in the life of a human being for an extended period of time, either on a conscious or a subconscious level, the delicate balance between the emotional and physical body is upset. The imbalance will be expressed by the physical body in some kind of dysfunction which causes pain in the end.

Anger

If we explore closely the term anger it has its roots in the meanings of distress and grief. The origins can also be traced in the German language where *"enghe"* literally means narrowing. The same is also found in the Indo European word *"angh"*, which not only means tight but also painfully constricted. We can see a relationship to anxiety as both words contain the meaning of narrowness.

What happens if somebody is in a constant state of repressed anxiety for a long period of time and then has no other alternative except to vent it in a violent outburst of anger. Anger on an emotional level is the manifestation of the same type of energy as the season spring. In winter time, which is a manifestation of the same type of energy as anxiety a plant would contract and reduce its life force to its very essence which is a seed. When spring comes this concentrated life force bursts out and begins to sprout. There is a perpetual movement within this cycle. Anger will explode at some point as a reaction to repressed anxiety.

The build up and explosion of anger can happen very quickly when one is under direct threat and this brief outburst will not harm the body in the long term, in contrast to anger that has slowly been built up and suppressed since childhood. A clear example is of a child growing up in a very strict and oppressive atmosphere. In many cases the parents want to fulfil their dreams through their own children and this often results in a permanent conflict, especially if the children do not live up to their expectations. Parents and teachers can put a lot of pressure on the children, bringing them into a constant state of anxiety and fear. Fear of not been loved or very often the simple fear of punishment will make children conform. Conflicts will arise as soon as their own expectations and needs differ from that of their parents. These children may rebel one day and free themselves to live according to their own vision of life. But what happens if one cannot find the courage to break free from such patterns? This state of anxiety will continue to affect one's professional and personal life. The fear of losing one's job or a partner may be stronger than the will to free oneself from such destructive conditions. As a result of this a person represses the anger which continues to simmer on a subconscious level. There are a number of ways that this suppressed energy will burst out one day. One possibility is that it will break out on a physical level, affecting the spine and other related back problems. When suppressed anger breaks out it will affect two different types of tissue, one of which is the ligament tissue. When ligaments running along the vertebra and crosswise between spinal processes show inflammation at their entries, it will cause permanent pain when there is any movement, for example, bending or twisting of the back. Pain restricting any movement often leads to a poor metabolism within the skeletal muscles and further degenerative changes within the spine.

To give us a better understanding of the function associated with anger let us look closely at how it appears in nature. Thunder and spring both represent an immense explosion of life energy, just as in spring when all the buds sprout in spring. It happens when the cosmic principle of contraction has reached its peak in winter and then suddenly expands. But what happens if this outburst occurs within the human body in a destructive form? One can imagine many possibilities, but what they have in common is that this anger will manifest itself as an inflammatory process. An inflammation has the same characteristics as anger; it has a basically expansive nature. An inflammation is characterised by the following factors: redness, heat, swelling, pain and the end result is the dysfunction of the body structures involved.

The second and an indirect impact of anger, affects the cartilage layer of the small joints between all the vertebra. This occurs indirectly because of suppressed anger. Imagine the shoot of a tree breaking through earth. This can be interpreted as a destructive act because the surface of the soil is damaged. In the same way, anger destroys cartilage once it becomes a destructive energy. Anger is not necessarily destructive, it is just a quality of energy. Only in cases of imbalance does anger turn destructive.

Once one has understood that degenerative changes within the spine are not only a physical phenomenon but have an emotional component, once we accept bodily change as a physical manifestation of an emotional imbalance or disorder, there is a much better chance to slow down the process of degeneration. Anyone who wants to overcome back problems needs to be ready to change as a whole being instead of just passively trying out a number of treatments and cures. Treatment may bring some relief to the luckier ones at least for a while. But back problems will occur again and again if the root causes of the problems are not eliminated. The back problems suffered by so many people are clear signals that something is wrong in their emotional life. Once this problem is addressed there can be long lasting relief from back pain.

Joy

In contrast to the two emotional states we have discussed so far, joy as an emotion is not harmful to the spine at all. Rather it is the absence of joy which may cause problems. Joy itself is a cure to disorders of all kinds, including back problems. We need to consider joy in this context because of its influence on the degree of tension that occurs within our skeletal muscles. Joy is described as a spontaneous inner emotional reaction to a pleasant situation, a person or to a memory. Joy can occur in a great number of feelings in varying degrees of intensity. It is expressed to others on a wide range of scale, from a smile to an elated cry or an exuberant outpouring of words. If we describe joy as having an expansive effect this is because a person motivated by joy is highly productive. Such enthusiasm, however, can have negative effects on the individual if it is too excess because they may not be aware of the strain on their system.

Seen from a biochemical perspective, joy is a result of a dopamine release within the brain through naturally rewarding experiences such as food, sex, use of certain drugs and the neuronal stimuli that are associated with them. Dopamine has a mutual influence on the mood of each individual. The moment one experiences a pleasant situation, like kissing or winning a game, this "happiness hormone" creates a feeling of being high and the motivation to reach such a state again and again increases. Addictions of any kind are the dark side of this phenomenon. A cell structure situated in our middle brain no bigger than the size of a pea is responsible for this. It is called the *nucleus accumbens* and works as the core of a rewarding unit within the limbic system of our brain. The receptors are found here which when stimulated are experienced as pleasure and satisfaction.

One way to increase the level of dopamine is through drugs is the use of so-called 'recreational' drugs such as amphetamines, cocaine or opiates. These affect a number of brain areas simultaneously and lead to a state of euphoria. Alcohol, nicotine and caffeine also stimulate the concentration of dopamine, but this affects only the *nucleus accumbens*. However, this "kick" does not last long because dopamine metabolises very fast and its production is reduced very quickly after a drug or stimulant has been taken. The desire to remain in a constant state of high may often result in drug addiction.

Dopamine was first discovered in the 1950s by the Swedish scientist *Arvid Carlsson*. He found out that this signal substance is necessary to control body movements. Dopamine is a *neurotransmitter* which means it has the ability to both activate and inhibit neuronal cells. It can transmit orders from the neuronal system to the skeletal muscles. There is a link between the level of dopamine release and muscular tension or relaxation. A lack of dopamine in the brain may lead to increased tension within the muscles which results then in all the negative effects we have discussed earlier. An increase in the level of dopamine is needed in order to release tension within the muscles. This is also true for the autochthon muscles interconnecting all the vertebra to each other.

In relation to the human body, especially to the spine and a number of problems occurring there, we can now observe a relationship between the degree of tension within the skeletal muscles and the level of dopamine. If a person often experiences joy it will help reduce muscular tension. Joy as an emotion possesses the power to rejuvenate a person from destructive influences such as stress and anxiety caused by job problems or difficult personal relationships. It is therefore essential to consciously reward oneself from time to time to keep the balance. It is not helpful to use drugs or alcohol to increase your dopamine level. Doing so will bring about other health problems in the long run related to the abuse, and additionally a suppression of the deep rooted problems which will surface again at a later stage. If one finds time for real relaxation it will lead to an increased capacity for a state of joy. This quality of relaxation can be experienced by going on regular walks in beautiful natural surroundings, by cycling or playing sports. All these physical activities will lead to good results as long as you avoid becoming fanatical, as this would lead to new problems instead of solving the old ones. Meditation is also very helpful, whether in the form of sitting and contemplating, or active meditation based on body exercises like Yoga or Tai Chi. Leading a well balanced social life is also important for bringing relaxation and joy. Meeting friends, enjoying a good meal together or doing activities with people you really like are vital for increasing the fun factor in your life. You can derive joy not only from leisure activities but also from doing any task which gives you satisfaction, such as a job you really like doing. For many people work is for earning money, nothing else. This is very unfortunate because a large part of life can be wasted doing boring work just for the sake of money, whether you like the job or not. Real life for many people takes place only on weekends and holidays. Is it any wonder then that we see an increasing number of people suffering from back pain related to their professions? This is not only because of heavy physical labour of blue collar workers or the bad body postures of desk bound employees, it is also because of the complete absence of joy at work. If this is so it is worthwhile to rethink your attitude towards work before your body reminds you to do so through severe episodes of back pain.

Sadness

We all feel sad sometimes. Much of art and poetry is inspired by melancholy. Sadness almost always accompanies a sense of loss. Sadness also helps us appreciate happiness. When there is a change of one's mood from sadness to happiness the contrast enhances your ability to realize the value of the state of happiness. When we experience acute sadness, the muscles of the throat constrict the salivary glands release a viscous fluid, repeated swallowing occurs, the eyes close tightly, and the lacrimal glands release tears. Sadness is a natural feeling which, if it is not felt, will remain in the domain of unresolved trauma clusters. As with other emotions, once it is felt it will go away. The avoidance of being able to feel sadness in the form of intense sobbing, grief and tears, makes you more prone to addictions of any kind, to develop psychosomatic symptoms, and to exhibit high levels of anxiety and erratic behaviour. Resist these feelings and it will be around forever, erupting periodically at inappropriate times as our body attempts to rid itself of associated trauma clusters.

In our spine, cartilage covers facet joints and it is also the material the fiber rings of the intervertebral discs are made of. Interestingly enough, problems like a prolapsed disc are very often seen in people suffering from difficult relationships between themselves and their partners. Men and women are equally affected by this phenomenon. Their problems with each other may arise from a number of different origins but there will always be an element of anger and sadness within them. If a couple falls in love and everything is going smoothly for them they experience a state of intense happiness and their world is filled with beauty. From a clinical viewpoint this occurs because of being permanently high on dopamine. But such a condition usually does not last long. After a period of time as the couple shares their daily routine together and the passion begins to ebb, different forms of conflict will begin to surface. These conflicts come from expectations about the partner which have not been fulfilled satisfactorily. These differences may be about sexuality, fidelity, raising and caring of children, and also financial difficulties or disagreements. One person will feel isolated within a relationship, especially if there is a lack of communication. The feeling that their personal needs have not been understood, supported or accepted by their partner creates sentiments experienced as loneliness. All these problems could easily be solved if the partners would speak about it. But often they are not listening to each other. This leads to a sense of resignation and desperation in loneliness and a permanent state of sadness. How such an emotional state will manifest into a physical disorder will depend on the general predisposition of a person. We are only looking at the spine. There are two main ways that tissue may be affected, and both have in common a state of permanent sadness which weakens connective tissue of any kind. One type manifests as a degenerative change which will result in a prolapsed disc in the end. The other ends up as inflammatory processes involving autoimmune problems such as *arthritis* and *athrosis*.

What are the effects on an individual of being in a state of permanent sadness? It creates a feeling of being powerless, weak and completely exhausted. If such conditions develop on a physical level we can easily understand what the impacts are on connective tissue like the fibrous ring of our intervertebral discs. In the long term they will wear out in the same way as if we were constantly overstraining it through physical pressure. The idea that an emotional state also expresses itself directly as a destructive bodily sensation may seem strange to some of us. It may be easier to accept a more indirect effect as it seen with anxiety. But there is a direct connection between relationship problems and prolapsed discs. This has been proven by a number of studies and statistics.

Depression

Depression can be both a trigger of back pain and a result of it. If you experience a persistently sad, anxious or "empty" mood or permanent feelings of hopelessness, pessimism, guilt, worthlessness and helplessness, you show clear symptoms of depression. This leads to a loss of interest in leisure time activities that you once enjoyed. You also tend to lose your interest in having sex. Individuals affected by depression have difficulties in concentrating, remembering things and making decisions; they feel slowed down and experience a state of low energy levels and constant fatigue. Some may suffer from insomnia or being wide awake early in the morning. In some cases they want to stay in bed for the whole day, feeling unable to get up. Depressive people often lose their appetite and as a result of this they lose weight; it can also have the opposite effect as they overeat and gain weight. Thoughts of death and suicide or suicide attempts are common in an advanced level of depression. Other typical characteristics of a depressive state are restlessness, irritability and persistent physical symptoms that do not respond to treatment, such as headaches, digestive disorders, and chronic pain.

If someone suffers severe back pain over a long period of time this person's movements will be greatly restricted. Then the purpose of their whole existence becomes concentrated on the one aim of overcoming this pain. The consequences will be a loss of quality of life until the whole situation looks hopeless, especially if every therapy has failed and the affected person has given up believing that there is any relief available. As soon as a very active person suffers from a prolapsed disc and is confined to bed for many weeks he is forced to examine his inner self. Often people in such a situation discover an inner emptiness that may lead them to experience anxiety and desperation. Suddenly their whole life seems to be senseless and may result in the state of a deep depression. If someone's self worth is defined only through his activities it will not be easy for such a person to accept these restrictions occurring in a worst case scenario as near paralysis. In severe cases of herniated disc any minute movement causes excruciating pain and the only way to avoid this is to have a complete bed rest for a minimum of three weeks. With orthodox medical treatment medicine such patients would be administered a concoction of medication containing painkillers and antidepressants. Antidepressants in such cases may help one to feel better for the moment but this is nothing more than a chemically produced illusion, an ineffectual attempt to trick the body's reaction on its path to a self destructive behaviour. It is not a solution to the real underlying issues.

A disorder of any kind within the body contains its own message. Disorders of any kind never occur without a reason and this reason is obvious in the case of a herniated disc. A disc prolapse may be a hard but efficient way to start feeling one's own body again. Feeling one's own body is the absolute prerequisite to developing the ability to face reality and to mature and grow from the challenges one encounters in life. One can look at being confined to bed as being given the time to contemplate one's life and how to fill up the emptiness in it. Instead of depending on antidepressants, people with a prolapsed disc need the qualified care of someone who can help them to rediscover the wealth of their inner world. This is the better way to save them from depression.

CHAPTER 3

Destructive Mental Patterns

Exploitation and Self Abuse

Overstretching and misusing our limited physical resources to meet our unrealistic expectations of life leads to the exploitation and self abuse of the body. By ignoring the needs of the body and not paying any heed to its early warning signals, we harm ourselves physically. By nature each individual's body is equipped with a limited amount of resources and abilities. These vary from one individual to another. Some are gifted in one area and have deficits in others. As humans are designed to live in groups, different skills are equally balanced through a division of labour between all the members of a community. Nowadays most people are forced to take on tasks that are totally incompatible to their nature. This kind of distribution forces many people to misuse their physical resources and destroy their own bodies. On the other hand there are others who voluntarily follow only their personal concept of life regardless of their real physical capacity.

What is your attitude towards your performance at work? What approaches do you have to your duties within your family and who defines them? Do you take into consideration that your physical resources are limited when you are thinking over this? Answering these questions honestly is the first step to understanding how much your mental patterns are responsible for your attitude towards your own body. These mental patterns often do not include one essential thing and this is respect. Respect is not such a popular notion any more within our society. The respect we show for each other as well as respect in the greater sense of using our resources in an intelligent way are now obsolete. Today the ones who are given the highest recognition and the ones who are making the most profit regardless of the damage to the environment, to others and least of all to oneself.

The desire for money or recognition or the longing for both have become so much more important than adhering to the basic laws of life. These laws are applicable to everything that lives within our world, whether it is a cod or a human body. There was a time when there was so much cod in the seas that the idea that they may die out one day would have been absolutely ridiculous. Generations of fisherman caught them, dried them to stockfish. There was enough stockfish to feed all the sailors at sea and enough cod to fry it and serve it as fish and chips to the people on land forever. Technologies in fishing have changed and now it is possible to find all the cod wherever they swim in the seven seas. They are caught regardless of whether their population is able to regenerate or not. This does not matter, only making more money does. If we continue to fish in this way the cod population will die out very soon. Everybody is aware of this development: the fishermen, the government and many consumers as well. Unfortunately this has not made any difference; they continue to ignore the warning signs as day by day the trawlers sail to catch as much cod as they can.

What will you do when you feel back pain the first time? Many people try to ignore it. They ignore it for as long as they can because being restricted by pain does not fit into their lifestyle. When back pain occurs we can make a simple calculation. This calculation includes the quality of our life as well as our ability to function in whatever we do. Ignoring back problems for as long as possible will drastically reduce both your life's quality and your ability to work to a minimum. It is hard to believe but a great number of people behave in this manner. To pretend to oneself as well as to others that everything is all right even if it is obvious that it isn't, is a very common trait. People behaving in this manner are not able to see any other way to manage their lives other than exploiting their own bodies as far as possible. They do not think about making any lifestyle changes as that would mean acknowledging the need to reorganize their life in such a way that would allow them to care for themselves. People may think they are being courageous but the truth is that it is very regrettable to behave like this.

Another common way to react to back problems is to ask an expert to sort them out. In most cases without any doubt this is the right thing to do. Unfortunately people often go for therapy with the purpose of continuing their old lifestyle after a successful course of treatment. This may work for a while. This is like someone who sees the warning light indicating that the motor oil in his car is low, and destroys the warning lights instead of checking the engine. There is a reason why a warning sign has flashed up – and there is a reason why you experience back pain. The reason is that something is going wrong within your body. And it is time to ask yourself some serious questions and to search for answers within your system. What most of us tend to do is to ignore the warning signals completely. Why do we fail to listen and respect the needs of our body? The answer to this lies in the views we have about what our own life should be like: Our image of a successful career and our picture of a happy family life. These ideas of success and happiness that we hold usually conform to those held by the society that we live in. We tend to neglect our own body. The body is viewed as nothing more than an instrument through which all our work can be done. If we continue with this attitude that our body (like the cod that continues to be caught) has a limitless capacity to be abused and exploited, than we have blinded ourselves to the reality of the situation. Continuing to follow these kinds of unrealistic ideas about life may in the end result in severe degenerative changes within the spine which could be irreparable.

Unfortunately most people only realize that they have allowed themselves to be exploited when it is much too late. This is especially true in the case of women who often take on multiple roles simultaneously. Besides a full time job, most women often raise their children singlehandedly even if there is a partner present. They continue to meet the remorseless demands of their children and spouses, often neglecting or ignoring the needs of their own bodies. Where will the children raised by such parents learn to respect the needs of their bodies or accept its limitations? It will not be from a father whose professional career takes precedence over family and who is often present only at breakfast, dinner and leisure time activities on the weekends. It will not be from a mother who attends to the needs of everyone else from day to night. How will children learn about self care and self respect from such parents?

Of course economic pressure exists. Of course one single person cannot change the surrounding conditions of our society all by himself but we can start to listen to our own bodies and find out where its limitations are. We can take the time to regenerate and accept this as an important part of our life instead of viewing our health as a bothersome duty. As long as we are not able to respect ourselves how can we ever manage to respect others?

Our back is a very good teacher which helps us to develop self respect on a physical level. By starting to listen to it we will learn how to use our physical capacities in an intelligent way. We can learn to stretch our limits if necessary without harming ourselves.

Mental Rigidity

By observing people closely when they move it is possible to get a lot of information about their personal characteristics. Movement patterns are a direct expression of the mental patterns which created them first. To understand this concept it is necessary to view the human being as a whole unit made up of inseparable components: the physical body, the emotions, the mind, and the spirit or the soul. All these components constantly interact with each other in a continuous process of learning through stimuli provided by the personal environment. These stimuli need not necessarily be of a pleasant nature but they are useful as they initiate many kinds of changes to our lives.

It is not easy for many of us to accept this fact straight away. Instead of being open and looking at all the possible opportunities we have to react to whatever problem we are facing, many of us tend to habitually take the well-trodden path which was established a long time ago. What was once successful is generally thought of as being successful forever, in the belief that what was once true will always be true. Thus, people try to control their lives with the aim of creating stability and security for themselves. Yet people who behave in this manner will have to pay an enormous price for their mental rigidity. Life offers countless opportunities to grow and by not taking up and integrating these new perspectives we fail to develop our personal wisdom. Such a parochial outlook is very common within our society and if you look closely at how people move when they are passing by you will immediately be able to identify people with an inflexible outlook, whose habits are set in stone. They are not flexible at all; they are as physically restricted as their views are about the world. It is amazing when we think of how these individuals would have been as children, just as curious and open minded as all children usually are. Their spine was as flexible as a bamboo stick and their ability to learn seemed limitless. They lived their lives as young children do, flowing blithely and bubbling like a young mountain stream. When did the moment come when this fluidity changed into a petrified state of near rigidity, and how did this happen? When were they stunted in this way?

Children learn by imitation and their first role models are their parents. The present concept of family life involves a group of three, four, sometimes five people. It is unusual nowadays for families to have more than three or perhaps four children. As a result children have no other choice except to take on patterns of movement and thought processes from their parents just as they will have done from their own parents. Specific family neuroses, a basic world view, preferences and animosities are passed from one generation to the next creating a typical family tradition. Though perhaps this is not applicable for everyone, for the vast majority this means containment, a filter through which we have learned to perceive and judge ourselves and the world. Other filters are implemented later through school and further educational systems when we train for a profession. This form of training often leads people to view the world narrowly through the eyes of their respective professions, for example as a plumber, a sociologist, a medical doctor. As people begin to identify themselves with their jobs they begin to lose a large part of their unique self and merge with their chosen professions.

A completely different structure of society can be found within the so-called primitive native people all over the world. They have also developed identification patterns based on their specific cultural, social and environmental conditions. The difference between our cultural view to theirs is found within their basic understanding of responsibility towards each other in their communities. To understand the impact this has on education let us have a closer view at their ideas of family life, for example those developed by the Plains Indians of Northern America. There, children were seen as not only belonging to their parents but as a part of the whole community. This made every adult feel responsible towards them. Children ate in the tipi wherever food was served and slept wherever they were tired. By living in such a community these children had a larger number of role models than those in a modern Western family. This was helpful in developing all the different personal components which are found within children so that they could achieve a more holistic understanding of their world. This would result in them having open and flexible minds.

In our society of so-called "experts", the view of the world does not only narrow because of being raised by a small family, it also narrows because as a successful professional you have to focus mainly on the subject of your own work. People sink into a psychological and physical impoverishment if they are unwilling to balance their lives. For example, to achieve a balance, white collar workers could take up physical sports to balance their desk-based work, while a blue collar worker would need mental stimulation in the form of learning a foreign language or playing a musical instrument. This is just one way to avoid becoming narrow and rigid in the mind and the body. When we look at the great number of sufferers of back pain and the kind of lifestyle they lead we find that their original self has been greatly reduced to a "something" which would fit a specific mould. There is a way of reviving all the forgotten components of a personality which have not been cultivated. We can easily gain access to our whole psychological potential but the access to our bodily potential depends on our present physical condition. It is very easy to regain this potential because it is only one step away from our consciousness.

To test the effects of how easily we can gain access to our body's full potential, read the following paragraph slower than your normal speed paying close attention to the text. There is no need to do the movements, you will feel the effects merely by focusing on a part of your body through reading this text.

Think of your right hand. Become aware of all the small bones within your five fingers, two in your thumb and three in all other fingers. These little bones are connected through little joints, one in the middle of your thumb, another one connecting your thumb to the metacarpal bone. Each of your fingers has two joints and one more connecting the finger to the metacarpal bone. Think of these bones and little joints one after the other, be aware of their presence and feel them as a part of your hand. You can bend each single joint of your fingers. Become aware how your fingers are connected to the metacarpal bones, think of how they build the framework of your right palm. From the base joints where your fingers meet the metacarpal bones become aware of how you can bend them up and down all together as well as one by one. You can circle your fingers one by one and they can be stretched to the side all together. Feel how your fingers are interconnected with your right wrist and be aware of it. Think of how your wrist can bend up and down; think of how it can bend from one side to the other. You can circle your wrist to the left and to the right, be aware of this movement.

Once you have finished reading this, compare how your right hand feels to the left one, compare the feeling of the right arm to your left arm. Isn't it amazing what happens if you simply put a little more awareness on something like your right hand? If we now apply this concept to a whole person it soon becomes obvious that our physical body has unlimited possibilities by being merely aware of its presence and of its function we can alter our consciousness to a point were we can influence it consciously.

This does not only work with our own bodies, altered awareness will also change our perception of other people as well as our perception of our whole environment. Being aware of our own body is the gate through which we can leave the cage of mental rigidness acquired from our education. Besides a lot of other benefits, these insights will be very helpful when we suffer from back problems. Once we have opened our minds, we are able to locate the blockages that are restricting us and we are able to trace them back to their origins. We will identify the physical origins as well as the problems which led to its creation. As a result we will be able to change not only a destructive lifestyle but also our physical condition. How this works is discussed in detail later. For the moment we will investigate a number of other mental patterns which separate us from the reality of life. Being isolated from the flow of life can lead to mental rigitity which in the long run will cause physical rigidness and will cause back pain.

Defensiveness

Some people experience the whole world as a hostile place. They are not able to trust anything or anybody and this creates a state of permanent stress within them. Stress is the origin of permanent muscular tension. It leads to movement and posture patterns which will result in the occurrence of several forms of back pain. Defensiveness is expressed in two main forms as posture and movement patterns. What they both have in common is that they affect primarily the thoracic area, the shoulders and the neck.

Reacting to any form of menace, either imaginary or real, is usually expressed through body postures which are either defensive or offensive. The defensive type of reaction would be to move the shoulders forward and to close the chest, simultaneously moving the neck like a tortoise would do. A person reacting defensively tries to protect his heart and chest. This posture does not need to be very exaggerated in order to affect the skeletal muscles on a long term. Even a slight but permanent tension in the trapezius – the big muscle covering nearly the whole back part of the chest up to the neck – is enough to create problems here. The muscles which lift the shoulder blades and those which turn the head from side to side are also affected by this posture, as are the breast muscles – the pectoralis – on the front of the chest. When they shorten and become weak because of habitual posture patterns, the back can become hunched, because the thoracic spine is not balance by the frontal muscles, which may lead to this deformity.

The offensive type of body posture is exactly the opposite of a defensive one. It is the classic stomach in and breast out posture which has been propounded over a long period of time as the correct one, especially for men. The shoulders are pulled backwards to push the chest out in front. Someone who assumes such a posture wants to create an impression of being superior so that the others can not come close to them. In this sense such a posture is an expression of defensiveness which affects the spine in many ways. Pulling the shoulders back all the time would mean stretching the spine to an unnatural position and building up a lot of tension in the neck. The whole hip girdle is affected because pushing out the chest out forces the buttocks to tense and this has a negative effect on the flexibility of the hips as well as on the lower back.

Many of us adopt these offensive or defensive postures to avoid being emotionally hurt. A defensive posture could have originated from experiencing feelings of constant rejection as a child. Our childhood experiences most often shape our attitude and views about life and in the long run will affect us physically. Children who have positive experiences with their parents and other adults within their family circle will most likely grow up to have a well balanced and open minded approach to the world around them. Unfortunately the number of adults who actually have this close personal relationship has become very small nowadays.

In our modern society, stress has become a permanent part of our lives, professionally and economically. Besides constantly worrying about these two aspects of life, many young adults see raising children as an additional strain. Being overloaded by all these responsibilities, these parents do not have enough time and energy left to invest in the personal development of their children, and these over-stressed parents withdraw further emotionally to protect themselves. The children cannot understand the reason for this withdrawal, all they experience is a rejection which is painful to them. If this situation continues over a longer period of time and there are no other adults present present to balance the situation for them, the children will react by holding themselves back. They build up an inner armour to avoid feeling pain. This leads to a state of defensiveness which will manifest itself as a destructive body posture causing back pain.

An offensive body posture is a different reaction to the same problem. It depends on a person's character how he will react to problems. Some people will try to protect themself by withdrawing and assuming a defensive posture, while others tend to assume an offensive position and posture to achieve their aims. In a defensive posture, an individual closes up his chest which is a physical expression of avoiding feeling others. The offensive posture closes the hip region and is a clear expression of not being able to feel oneself. How can someone who is unable to feel oneself be able to feel others? It is virtually impossible. These people will have a tendency to follow their idea of being successful without caring about others around them. Others are mainly seen as useful tools or as obstacles which have to be overcome. Those on the offensive will exhibit the same behaviour towards their own body. As long as their body supports the fruition of their goals they do not care about its health and wellbeing, and when a problem begins to occur they tend to ignore it for as long as possible. If this no longer works then they look for an expert to solve their problems for them. They will never think of changing their own behaviour pattern which has led to physical problems in the first place because they are unable to listen to their body.

To overcome defensiveness patterns which are the underlying causes for spinal disorders and back pain, the whole body needs to go through a process of re-education to dissolve destructive posture patterns and change the psychological states which first led to them. One way is to create a state of relaxation which will enable an individual to rediscover the whole range of his body's flexibility. One technique is to make him aware of his habitual action of pulling his shoulders to the front whenever he feels an emotion. This can easily be done. He has to only lie on the floor and observe which parts of his body are touching the floor. He should also check if both sides of the body feel equal or if there is a pain or tension felt somewhere. This will be described in detail in a following chapter, along with exercises which can be done to change such postures. Practicing these exercises regularly will not only dissolve muscular tension, but it will also help to change the psychological state of a defensive reaction.

A change in self perception automatically creates a change in the perception of the personal environment. Increasing one's flexibility leads to a wider range of perceptions and will result in new perspectives. Increased self awareness leads to greater self - confidence which is helpful in overcoming rejection. People who once reacted defensively or offensively will be able to feel that they are no longer isolated and may reach a point where such reactions are not necessary. With this realisation comes the ability to cure their back problems from its origins.

CHAPTER 4

The Column of Light in the Temple of Men

The Concept of Life Energy

Back pain is in many cases the result of an interaction between mental and emotional states which finally manifest as physical problems. In a previous chapter we learned how emotions can be interpreted in different ways. The result of an important experiment conducted by *Schachter & Singer* mentioned in Chapter 2 defines emotions as an arousal of nerve endings which is only given a meaning through the interpretation of the situation. The concept of emotion is different in oriental medicine. *Five Element Theory* says that each emotional state is a manifestation of a specific cosmic principle. Traditional Chinese Medicine tells us that good physical health depends on the balance between the five elements. When there is an imbalance the flow of qi or chi life energy through the body is blocked. Qi life energy interconnects the physical, emotional and mental part of a human and is essential for the health of each individual. When we can influence the quality and movement of qi energy, we possess an instrument which allows us to access all aspects of a disorder so that we can heal any problem from its source instead of just treating the symptoms.

The idea of Qi or life energy is not exclusive to the Chinese, this idea of an aura or an energetic body is present in many different cultures around the world throughout history. It is described in Buddhist scriptures and in the much older Indian chakra system. In Christianity, however, the idea of an energetic body was eclipsed very early and the glorioles and aureoles faded into symbols of a non-earthly sacredness.

African people such as the *Karanga* and the *Maschona* from

Zimbabwe still preserve their knowledge about the shadow, an invisible body which exists together with the physical body. The invisible body is called *Nwega* which means "white shadow" or soul. They believe that this shadow leaves the physical body during sleep, when death occurs or when one is in a state of trance. *Nwega* possesses its own sense organs which are thought to be much more efficient than those of the physical body.

Among the *Kahunas* – the sages of the native Hawaiian people – there is a tradition of three energetic bodies that humans possess. *Unihipili* is the subconscious body, *Uhane* the conscious body, and the *Aumakua* who is a kind of super conscious parental self. All these three exist independently of each other connected only by a life string.

Australian Aborigines have in their tradition that at the moment when death occurs the non-physical component of an individual will divide into three parts. There is one soul which has a relationship to the place of birth and to the spirit beings of the animal and plant kingdom who are connected through a blood line. These nourish a person throughout their lifetime. To the Aborigines the soul of the clan is connected to the ancestors who exist in *"Dreamtime"* and to the land of the dead in heaven which is located by each clan in a specific constellation of stars. Finally there is the *"Trickster soul"* which understood as the "ego soul" connected to a specific place, to partners, children and relatives, as well as to personal belongings like clothes, jewellery or tools. This type of soul carries a potential danger because it is not easy for the Trickster soul to accept the death of the individual which can result in the state of being trapped in this existence even after death.

The Native Americans recognized the importance of light and have therefore given the number One on their sacred medicine wheel to the sun. All life is created from sunlight and each single atom in our sun system is made from this energy.

The idea of non-physical bodies consisting of light is a very old one. The ancient Egyptians knew of ten different bodies and one of these, known as *Khu*, which means shining clearly, was the body of light, which was believed to continue to live on after one is physically dead.

According to the neo-Platonian Greek philosopher Damaskios, the soul is an eternal shining vehicle which is similar to a star. As long as someone is alive this eternal star will be enclosed within the physical body or only within the head. Countless pictures of religious figures of gods and demons in China, Tibet, India, ancient Egypt, Greece and Rome are depicted with a shining aura around them. Others have a shining aura just around their heads, as in Christianity were this halo is very common among the saints.

The life energy of a human, his bio photonic field or aura has been described in detail by the Indian and Tibetan Tantrics. *Tantrism* is a religious system which has its origin in India. The name comes from *Tantras*, the holy books of the *Schaktas*, the worshippers of Shakti, the female goddess of creation. According to the teachings of the *Tantras* the *Chakras*, a Sanskrit word and means literally "wheels of light", are organs of this body of light, situated along the vertebral column. The chakras are closely linked to all important neuronal centres and to all the ductless glands of the endocrine system.

From the Tibetan tradition comes the idea of a luminous *"diamond body"*. This is hidden in the material body and one is only able to look at it as a shining halo when someone falls into a deep trance at the highest level of meditation. The Chinese Taoists also describe light emitted by human being as having darker colors for a lower level of consciousness and brighter colors for a higher one. All these have their basis in the observations of mystics in Eastern religions, and in more contemporary times of clairvoyants here in the West, who in altered states of consciousness are able to see a delicate shining aura of light around people. From the brightness, the colors and the structure of this aura they draw conclusions about physical, emotional, mental and spiritual state of a person. From the experiences of ancient clairvoyants comes the traditional concept that not only the bodies of gods and angels consist of pure light but that the human body is an expression of light because its material is made from light. Surprisingly this matches accurately with the findings of the present day physicists.

Light and Information

Light is defined as electromagnetic radiation. The visible light is only one out of all the different forms of electromagnetic radiation. Electromagnetic radiation is classified according to the frequency of the wave; these include, in order of increasing frequency, radio waves, microwaves, terahertz radiation, infrared radiation, visible light, ultraviolet radiation, X-rays and gamma rays. Light emitted from living cells consists of bio photons. Each living cell emits a low intense radiation of bio photons.

This kind of phenomena is not only seen in human beings but each living creature emits some kind of light. From this point of view we can say that everything in the universe is alive. To define animals and plants as living things and rocks and water as non-living is erroneous. They have been essential for human life to come into being so how can this considered as dead matter? We consider these so called non-living things as dead matter because we do not yet have the technical know how to measure and prove their vitality. However, we do have the technology to see the light emitted by organic cells. Biophysicists can objectively see this phenomenon on the screen of their machines and they call it "*bio photons*". Each living cell emits a low intense radiation of bio photons. Bio photons are "*lightquants*", which are the same as those emitted by the sun but at a much lower intensity. Lightquants have some amazing characteristics. They are continuous waves from the sun and at the same time wherever we look at them they are particles. This characteristic is the reason why we are able to see these lightquants. *Gurwitsch*, a Russian physicist who lived in the early 1920s, described this phenomenon as "Light emitted by the living" and called it *"mitogenetic radiation"*. *Popp*, a German physicist from Freiburg, who is a leading authority in this specific field, calls it "ultra low cell radiation".

Where does this radiation come from?

There is an interaction between light and material. When a photon hits an atom in which the electrons move on courses with different energy levels, the energy of the photon initiates the movement of an electron from an inner lower level to an outer higher level course. The duration of this stimulation is in the sphere of nano and microseconds. When it is finished the electron moves back to its original level because of the gravitational forces in the nucleus. The energy which has moved it before, cannot get lost, so it is emitted again as a photon, a biophoton.

All together the bio photons emitted by single cells build up a field of light. For example, all the liver cells build up a specific field of bio photons which is energetically equivalent to the physical organ. The sum of all the specific field of organs and tissues of different qualities together forms the *"aura"*. This aura represents the vitality of the body from which it is emitted. To illustrate this fact let us look at a method developed by Alfred Popp where the quality of food is investigated by measuring the emission of light. By measuring the photons emitted from a piece of meat, from a fruit or some vegetables it can be proven if it is fresh or if it had been chemically treated or had gone through a degree of radiation.

The origin of all the light on earth is the sun. A radiation field consisting of sunlight and electromagnetic fields in the biosphere like the electromagnetic field of the earth builds a matrix for the structure of matter. All matter which comes into being, atoms, molecules, cells and also whole organisms are a result of the interaction between sunlight and the earth's electromagnetic field. All of them are shaped through the radiation field and therefore they have exactly those structures and dimensions which fit in this radiation field.

How does this electromagnetic interaction affect our health? Its impact becomes clear when you compare the influence of different surroundings on our state of mind and relaxation. When you compare a walk through a beautiful forest or along the beach you will feel different effects to that of a walk through a shopping mall where you are subjected to artificial light and air conditioning. Seen from physical point of view, both the natural surroundings and the man-made ones consist of electromagnetic radiation. The structure of this radiation interacts with the field of the electromagnetic structure of your body. This will in turn lead to a transfer of information which will shape your own energy field and in the long-term create changes within your physical body.

A similar effect can also be seen in the food we consume. What we eat is not only the carbohydrates, proteins, vitamins and mineral traces which nourish us but there is also the light structure from the food which communicates and influences our body's light structure. Depending on the information we receive, the energy from the food helps to stabilize our own system or in the cases of processed and poor quality food, it will destabilize our body's light structure and make us ill. Many of us feel that we are affected by the radiation emitted by cell phones, computers and other electronic equipment. Studies have been done to show the impact of this sort of radiation on the human system as well as the mutations induced by radiation in human and animal cells.

When we take into consideration that every living cell within our body is permanently emitting photons, we can find different structures of light manifesting as different organs and tissue structures. All of them interact with each other and build up an energy field which is our light body. This body of light communicates continuously with our environment. This light structure is a matrix in which our cells grow. When this light structure is intact it means that we have healthy tissue structures. Considering that most of our body's cells renew themselves it is clear how essential an intact light structure is for our physical health. This is not only because of the growth of new cells but also because this light structure controls all our body functions. There are sextillions of biochemical reactions within our body every second, neither the brain nor the hormone glands have the capacity to organise them all. There must be a form of intercellular communication which makes our bodies function as a unit instead of an unorganised cluster of cells. This communication is done by the light emitted from cells which transfers the information between them so that they can coordinate their biochemical activities.

If somebody becomes ill, dramatic changes take place within their light field. We can say that the light structure of a body is in disharmony. When the balance of the electromagnetic field is disturbed, the cells cannot properly renew themselves and the steering system of all biochemical body functions does not work accurately any more resulting in the destruction of tissue.

We have learned that spinal disorders and problems of tissue degeneration are not only due to direct physical exertions but also involve other aspects such as stress, poor diet of junk food, and a sedentary lifestyle, as well as other underlying reasons of a psychological nature such as emotional or mental states of imbalance. All these factors will distort the light body of an individual. This is the missing link between all origins of back pain, both physical and psychological.

With this insight we have a tool which will enable us to treat all the origins of back pain simultaneously. To cure any disorder at an early stage and to prevent it from becoming worse, someone can help themself through specific exercises. In cases of severe back problems, treating the light body directly will be a very powerful and efficient method. The key to being successful in this is clearly to restructure the distorted light body, but how can this be done?

The first step is to develop an awareness of the kind of feeling a specific surrounding or situation is giving to us. Your perception between a walk through the forest and a ride on the subway will be different because of the varying "electromagnetic" input. Once you have developed an awareness of this you can start to observe yourself and how you react to places and people, what strengthens you and what drains and weakens you. This kind of information is given to you by your light body and it is always available to you. Later you will learn that the perception of light structures is possible with each of your sense organs. We can feel life energy kinaesthetically and also we can literally see it. This is not a miracle, it is a natural gift inherent in all of us. Our own light body is the matrix for our physical body that means we not only have physical sense organs but the same organs are made of "light". All we have to do is to reactivate those areas of our brain which are able to give us a conscious image of light structures. To move our body in a specific way will help us to recover and strengthen our light body which will in turn strengthen and protect our physical body. Once we have learned to create light patterns through movement and are able to perceive them, we will also be able to restructure the light bodies of others. How all this can easily be done will be explained in detail later.

The Snake Within our Body

The shape of the spine is similar to the shape of a snake. This is one of the reasons why the spine is thought of as the "snake within our body". Most people have an irrational fear of snakes and generally serpents do not have a good image at all. In Christianity the snake symbolises evil and temptation. However, the snake is a revered symbol in many cultures. In ancient Greece the snake symbolised healing abilities – hence the caduceus coil of modern medicine and the Hippocratic oath. And to ancient Egyptians snakes represented wisdom and enlightenment. This is the reason many deities including the Egyptian Pharaohs had the image of the head of a snake on their forehead which represents the third eye. It meant that the full potential of a being had unfolded when the snake appeared there.

The spinal column has an outstanding role within a human being's body of light. It is not only the central axis for all of our movements but is also very important for any form of exercise that aims to harmonize and balance the structure of our light body, as is the case with Tai Chi and yoga.

The spine is also essential for directing all neuronal impulses from the brain to the organs and extremities and vice versa. In the Chinese tradition the intervertebral discs have an additional role. They are an important reservoir of chi or life energy. To sum up, we can say that the spine holds together our whole body, the material one as well as the body of light.

The spine is divided into the cervical, the thoracic and the lumbar regions. We can find patterns here which can be used as an entrance to influence the light body. In the neck area, the seven vertebra of the cervical spinal column repeat the system of the seven main chakras. Each chakra is situated along the whole spine and represents a special frequency of life energy which is clearly expressed by the color of the light emitted by them. Each specific frequency performs a specific function within the body of light and manifests itself as a body function related to specific organs and tissue qualities.

The twelve vertebra of the thorax remind us of the twelve signs of the zodiac. The lumbar five is repeated twice by the sacrum and by the coccyx. The five represents the self on the sacred wheel of the Native Americans and correlates to the navel in the centre of the lumbar area as the energetic centre of a human body. In the Taoist concept of *Five Elements* this area is seen as the crucial centre of the abdominal cavity where all elements merge together. The sacrum has eight holes which are seen by the Taoists as being related to the eight powers on their medicine wheel the *I Ching*. Taoists understand these holes as absorbing stellar energy from the Great Wagon. This energy moves up to the brain and merges with the energy of the polar star in the vertex of our skull. These concepts are similar to the Indian yoga concept of raising the *Kundalini* energy. *Kundalini* is a Sanskrit word meaning "coiled up" or "coiling like a snake". The teachings of the Hindu Tantra depict the Kundalini energy as a snake which lies rolled up in the sacrum of the lower spine. In this tradition, Kundalini is said to rise upward through the various centres until it reaches the crown of the head, resulting in a union with the Divine. This is pictured as a snake winding along the spine into the brain symbolising the complete unfolding of all vital and spiritual powers which are inherent in an individual.

Although the Indian concept is in many ways similar to the Chinese system of the *Five Elements* it is very different to the cyclic structure postulated by the Taoist. The Indian concept describes a vertical rise where the energy is transformed to a "higher" frequency to fulfil more advanced functions from one centre to the next. This is like going through the different stages of evolution and reaching a more advanced state of consciousness up to the state of individual enlightenment. Often the lower chakras are thought of as having a lower level of consciousness because of their association to the libidinous and animalistic part of a human being. These kind of judgmental and hypocritical viewpoints create problems as chakras should not be classified as "higher" or "lower" in this sense. They are equally and insepa-rably connected. The complete spiritual development of a human being is only possible if each of the chakras produces clear light. This will only work when the "higher" ones receive the vital energy and information to be grounded by the "lower" ones and to transform the rising energy to another frequency and color.

The hip belt, the sacrum and the link between the fifth vertebra and the sacrum are all situated in the first chakra region. The first chakra emits red light and represents the instinct to survive and is associated with our sexual organs. The sexual organs represent the reproduction function and also include the cellular renewal within a human body. It is the evolutionary state of reptiles – which can regenerate parts of their body. Aging and degenerating changes can be understood as being the result of an undersupply of the light body in this specific frequency. The lack of red within the light body has a consequence on the electromagnetic field which gives a shape for the growth of cells. It is no longer able to transmit the information needed for a proper reduplication of cells. They will become damaged and may appear as degenerated tissue or in worst case scenario as cancer cells.

Seen from another perspective these same phenomena become clear when we take into consideration that physical movement is one of the main sources of creating the red frequency within our body. A sedentary lifestyle is one of the main reasons for aging and degenerative changes within our spine. Physical movement is important to generate light on the red frequency and to bring it into the system as the base energy on which all other frequencies depend. The hip belt, the sacrum area and the lumbar also need to be adequately flexible. If these regions are not as flexible as they should be it will have a negative impact on the whole spine which will begin to stiffen slowly. As a result of the restricted flexibility the upper parts are not energetically charged so they are unable to work properly. This has a negative impact not only on the spine but also on the organs and the body functions related to the segments with restricted flexibility.

If we want to heal the spine we have to be conscious about the importance of the hip and lumbar region and its impact on the rest of the spine. These regions have to be included first in any healing treatment and to apply appropriate exercises to revitalise it.

Considering the great number of prolapsed discs occurring between the fifth lumbar vertebra and the sacrum we can say that there is a direct link between prolapsed disc problems and the inaccessibility of the life force of red light emitted by the first chakra which is defined as the basic and essential life energy.

Transformation of Life Energy

In Tantra, transformation of life energy takes place when the kundalini uncoils and starts to rise from the sacrum area to the brain. It transforms as it moves through the seven main chakras. This transformation manifests itself as a specific function within the body of light. For example the function of the first chakra is to manifest an individual's physical body and to give the person the skills of self-perception. It depends on the "openness" of each chakra for it to evolve to its full potential. In fact as long as one is alive there is no chakra we can point to as being closed or opened. It is the quality of the spin of the chakra as to whether the kundalini can be transformed to a clear and bright light. If the spin of a chakra is disturbed it will produce light on its specific frequency but this light will be restricted in its quality. What this means is that the color emitted is not be as clear and bright as it should be. The disturbance of a chakra's spin has different origins. It may indicate an organic dysfunction in one of the organs associated with a specific chakra and/or a general lack of kundalini energy. As soon as the first chakra is not spinning properly the support for the upper chakras becomes insufficient. Any dysfunction of a chakra can be located directly on the spine and in many cases it can also be corrected from there.

The second chakra is situated around the belly button at the front and between the second and fourth lumbar vertebra along the spine. The rising kundalini reaches the chakra from the front and leaves it enriched with the frequency of orange through the back. If the chakra is spinning properly then a bright and clear orange light should be emitted from it. The color orange represents the evolutionary stage of fish and amphibians; the organs associated with the second chakra are the intestines and the lymphatic glands which are an essential part of the human immune system.

If the first chakra represents our ability to feel ourselves, the ability to feel others is represented by the second chakra. Our emotional life is attributed to the function of the second chakra. Earlier we learned the impact our emotions have on our spine and about a number of related problems that arise there. Is it any wonder when we discover now that strong stomach muscles are an essential precondition for the correct spinning of the second chakra. The stomach muscles play a very important role as they give the whole spine a kind of backing. This is another example of the sophisticated interaction between our body functions and our emotions. Such an interconnection is not only a physical reality but it is also found within our electromagnetic body of light.

The third chakra is situated at the back between the first lumbar and the ninth thoracic vertebra. In the front we find its centre around the lower end of the sternum. The kundalini moves into the third chakra through the back and leaves it by the front. The color emitted from this chakra should be a bright and clear yellow. As an evolutionary stage the third chakra represents the birds. The function of all the organs which are associated with the third chakra is an analytic one. The liver and the gall break down fat, the pancreas which is one of the glands assigned to this chakra breaks down sugar. The stomach transforms everything we eat to chyme and the kidneys separate pure water from uric acid and protein residue.

It is because of this analytic function that the third chakra is associated with our mental ability; this frequency stands for our reasoning power as well. There should be a good balance between our emotions and reasoning otherwise our lives will be diminished in quality. What the drama queen and a pure rationalist have in common is that they deny some essential parts of themselves so they can find neither harmony within them nor an opportunity for further spiritual development.

On a physical level the spiritual development is closely connected to the flexibility of our spine. If the lumbar and hip areas are not physically in tune and are not as flexible there will be not enough energy for the higher chakras to open to their full potential. In the case of the third chakra this can be illustrated when we compare the learning curve between two pupils: one who is sporty and the other who is not. A number of studies have proven that the one who is sporty will have the ability to grasp and retain their knowledge better than those who are inactive. Seen from the angle of the body of light this means that pupils who are doing exercise regularly will result in an increase of their intellectual capacity. Physical movement helps to metabolise all the additional adrenalin which is created when we focus mainly on intellectual work. This is one more example of how the balance between our chakras becomes reality on a physical level.

The 4th chakra is situated between the first and the eight thoracic vertebras at the back and along the sternum at the front. The kundalini moves in through the front of the chest and out of the back. There are a number of colors associated with this chakra. This chakra functions as a connecting link between heaven and earth. Some ancient traditions tell us that it is the red of the first chakra representing the earth and the white of the seventh chakra representing the heaven which is blended to pink within the fourth chakra, the heart chakra. A well known symbol which depicts this idea is the Star of David where the triangle of the three "earthly" chakras points upwards, and the triangle of the three "heavenly" chakras triangle points downwards. In the centre of both we find the Heart chakra, which is the fourth chakra, as the interconnecting link between them. Interestingly, this old Egyptian and Hebrew symbol also contains the idea of balancing poles as in the yin and yang symbol of the Chinese. It expresses the eternal balance between these two poles by portraying an upward movement of the "lower" chakras and a downward movement of the "higher" ones. These reverse movements of energy are an important concept to remember when we later focus on some exercises which can be done to manage the flow of kundalini within our spine.

The color of the fourth Chakra is also described as a lush green with a golden core in its centre. The associated evolutionary stage is that of mammals, the associated organs are the heart and the lungs and the thymus is the corresponding gland. These organs are enclosed by the rip cage which protects them. The thoracic part of the vertebra is the one which is by nature the least flexible of all. On the upper part of the chest we find the shoulders and directly connected to them are our arms which also belong to the fourth chakra. The legs as extremities belong to the first chakra and move our whole body. The arms and especially the hands are those parts of our body which touch others. We receive sensual impressions as a resonance by touching, hugging, stroking, holding hands or by laying our hands on others. These impressions are described as the "second feeling" compared to the "first feeling" or "gut feeling" we receive from the second chakra. This is the instinctive emotional reaction to others or to a specific situation. The second feeling comes only after there is an interaction involving others and we then make the decision as to whether we want to accept someone into our heart. Following this thought we can understand the specific function of the fourth chakra as the place where we make decisions to retain connection to someone or something.

From the back of the chest the kundalini continues to rise and enters the fifth chakra through the neck. After being transformed again hopefully with the addition of a bright and clear frequency of light blue the kundalini leaves this chakra from the front at the throat. At this point the kundalini has transformed to the spiritual stage .The evolutionary stage of the fifth chakra represents the human being. Its function is communication which is made possible through its associated organs: the ears allow us to hear; the tongue and the throat give us a voice. Having a voice means having the ability for self expression that is speaking and singing.

The flexibility of the seven cervical vertebras of the neck is vitally important. Depending on the mobility of the neck area and that of the tongue we are able to access the flexibility of the whole body. If the neck and the tongue are tight we are often restricted in many other parts of our body. Stiffness and inflexibility of the neck is often related to the limited and narrow outlook we have of life and of our own potential. Considering how the seven vertebras of the cervical spine reflect the seven main chakras it is no surprise to see many people suffering from neck problems. They do not allow their kundalini to rise and keep their chakras closed and this becomes mirrored in degenerated cervical vertebrae.

The sixth and the seventh chakra are both situated within the head. The sixth chakra is associated with the pineal gland and our ability to see. This includes not only the physical sense of seeing but also the ability of the body of light to see, which means being clairvoyant and literally seeing the life energy. The color associated with the 6th chakra is violet; but this can only come into being if there is enough red from the first and enough light blue from the fifth chakra to get an appropriate blend of violet. If we have not developed all the chakras below we will not have access to the powers of the sixth chakra or the so-called "third eye". There are only very few individuals who are able to reach such a state of complete evolution of their spiritual powers. Most of us tend to think that such gifts are supernatural. They are not! The key to making them available to all of us is to work with our spine which will reawaken the snake within our body. This will not only increase our physical health but will also solve our back problems. We will also be able to reach our full natural potentials as a human being. How we obtain this potential will be the content of the second part of this book.

PART TWO

How to Help Yourself

CHAPTER 5

Perception and Self Awareness

Appearance and Reality

All information about the concepts of the *Five Elements* as well as all those concerning the transformation of the kundalini through each chakra along the spine is not worth a dime as long as we try to understand these ideas only through the intellect. What these two concepts, together with a number of other ancient traditions, have in common is the symbolic representation of the vital processes of life. We will never be able to fully understand the mysteries of life but what we will be able to do is experience life. These vital processes of life depicted by the ancient mystery schools are a living reality within our own body.

If we want to integrate this kind of information into our daily life we have to learn to listen to our body. When we begin to increase our self awareness we will come into closest contact with the most powerful teacher we will ever have access to: our own body. This is not only extremely helpful in improving our state of health but it is also the most efficient way to grow spiritually.

Most of us have a total lack of self awareness. When we compare the lifestyle of today's western society to that of our neolithic ancestors we can see clearly how much the social and cultural conditions have changed. The only thing which has not completely changed since then is the human body. We are still built to walk about twenty miles a day to gather food. We are equipped to act and react instinctively to any situation within a natural surrounding. This works perfectly as long as we live closely connected to our environment and understand and accept ourselves as being a part of nature. Unfortunately over millennia we humans have separated ourselves from nature.

Our ability to create abstract ideas has no doubt brought a lot of benefits to humankind but on the other hand it has resulted in the mind becoming more dominant. We have lost touch with our physical body. Unaware of this dichotomy, our mind and body have begun to lead parallel lives. A typical symptom is the obsession to fill our minds with trivia and keep it constantly busy. We have a whole range of stimuli to occupy it such as magazines, radio, television and computers. For some it is a real torture to just sit without having distraction on a short ride on the train. As a contrast one needs to only observe how the Native people in America sat and waited for hours and days to get their rations from the government executives of the reservations. This endless patience of the Indians had been misinterpreted as them being dull and lazy.

Keeping the mind constantly filled is not reality. Our very physical existence is reality. What has been natural to the so-called primitive people who are still connected to the neolithic origins of human behaviour has become a subject of re-education to us living in a modern world. The first step to reunite ourself with the powers of life is to become aware of our own body. We need to understand and accept our physical body as being a temple or a cathedral where the mysteries of the divine are physically manifested. Balancing our body and mind as one is a precondition for unveiling the meaning of life for each human being.

This effort to link mind and body will help us to overcome a great number of disorders. In many cases it is nothing but a signal by our body to indicate that we are losing touch with our spiritual self and are going in the wrong direction. This is especially true in cases of back problems when we look at the spine as the circuit of kundalini energy. Whenever problems occur in the back we need to understand that they are a physical manifestation of an energy blockage created by our ignorance of ourselves which hinders us from developing our full potential.

Developing Inner Awareness

The times when you suffer from any kind of back pain are exactly those moments when you become aware of your physical body probably more than you have ever been before. You are forced to perceive your physical reality. There is no way out and you have the choice to deny your problems or try to cure them. Would curing in this instance mean taking medications, having treatments to overcome the back pain with the aim of continuing your present lifestyle? Or would it mean endeavouring to create a balance between all aspects of a human: your physical body, your emotional life, your mind and your soul. In cases of severe back problems you will have to seek professional help, but at the same time you have to begin taking responsibility for your wellbeing. The first step is to observe your pain. Get into a relaxed position and take a closer look inside yourself. Where exactly is the spot which gives you discomfort? If you can locate it then you can start to explore the parts of your body which are also involved. Where does the pain radiate? Which parts are restricted in flexibility? Which kind of movement is painful? From this point you can start to practice specific therapeutic body and awareness exercises which are described later. As an excellent preparation you will be shown a number of general exercises which aim to develop your inner awareness. These exercises can be done alongside the more specific ones. They will help to identify and solve problems before they occur physically. If you are a therapist, these exercises will help to increase your ability to identify the problem areas and help you to understand how they are interconnected in your patients.

Whether you are a patient or a therapist, the first two exercises will bring you into close contact to your body of light. To keep it simple, focus only on one specific tissue of your physical body: your bones. When you have mastered this stage you will later be able learn to intensify this work until you are able to perceive all the different forms of tissue and its interactions. This is important when you want to practice the more advanced specific therapeutic exercises for your back.

The third exercise introduced in this chapter will enable you to consciously control the flow of energy along your spine.

Once you start to practice them it will take a while until you become familiar with these exercises. In the beginning it will take you about twenty minutes to go through each of them. After about three weeks of daily practice you will only need a few minutes to do these exercises and derive the same effect. You can practice them before you go to bed or in the morning, whenever it is convenient for you.

It is important that these exercises should be done in a peaceful surrounding without any disturbances at first, so that you can easily keep your focus on the exercise. Later when you have built up a higher level of awareness you will be able to practice them wherever you want: on a train ride, during your lunch break, whenever you want to relax and recharge yourself. It does not matter if you sit upright or lie flat on your back when you are practicing these exercises. What is important is that you find a position where you feel most comfortable and then begin doing the exercises.

Two Exercises for Increasing Inner Awareness

Exercise 1

This exercise is the first step on the path to reunifying your mind and body. Following this path will enable you to heal yourself first and maybe later to heal others. Reunification of mind and body occurs once you have learned to connect your physical body to your body of light. The moment you focus your awareness on a specific part of your body you will literally feed it with energy. Practicing this awareness exercise at an advanced level will reawaken all the hidden potential of your personality which you have never had access to or even realized that they existed. Each of this manifests itself physically somewhere in your body.

We start with the bones because they are easy to identify as they are the most "material" and solid part of your body. This exercise will strengthen your bones and help you to accumulate life energy.

Assume a position where you feel most comfortable. You can either sit upright on the edge of a chair or if this is not possible you can support your back by leaning against the back of a chair. If you are sitting upright do it without creating any tension along your back. You can also do this exercise by lying flat on the floor or on your bed and support your head with a flat cushion. If you have problems with your lumbar spine you should use a cube to support your legs and to relieve your lower back of any tension. If a cube is not available you can also use a cardboard box of a suitable size and cover it with a blanket. If there are no lumbar problems then the knees should be supported by rolling up a blanket and placing it under the knees.

Place your hands on your upper legs if you are sitting. Or if you are lying down, place them along your body. Breathe in and feel the air moving through your nose into your body. Breathe out and feel the air leaving your body in the same way. Repeat this six times while breathing normally all the time.

Move your toes up and down a few times then stop and relax. Become aware of your right big toe and focus on the little top bone inside. This top bone is linked to a little joint. Become aware of this joint and now move your focus to the next little bone which connects your whole toe to another joint. Through this joint the whole toe is linked to the metarsal bone which is a part of the ball of your foot, become aware of this part of your foot's osseous inner composition. Now imagine an up and down movement of the right big toe. Imagine this movement is so real that you can feel as if you are moving it physically. Now repeat this part of the exercise one by one with each of the toes of your right foot. When you have finished, move all your toes together up and down – doing all this only in your imagination.

Become aware of all the five metarsal bones within the ball of your right foot. Think of them as being linked to the five other little cubic bones which make up the arch of your foot. Focus now on your heel bone and feel it being there. Then feel all the bones of your foot simultaneously.

Focus now on your right ankle, becoming aware of how your ankle links to your lower leg and to your foot. In your imagination move your right ankle up and down. Turn it to the left then to the right. Imagine moving your ankle in a circle in both clockwise and anticlockwise directions. Focus intensively on all these movements in your imagination until you can feel actually the movements without really doing them.

Next become aware of the two bones in your lower leg. The bigger one is the tibia which is connected to the fibula. At the upper end of your lower leg is your knee. Focus your attention there and once again bend and straighten your lower leg in your imagination.

Next focus on the big bone in your upper leg and feel its connection to the knee. Move your awareness up to the upper end the femur which has the form of a sphere. This sphere is connected to the socket of the hip joint. Now in your imagination move your leg in all the directions as far as your hip joint allows. Move your leg forward and back, move it to the side and rotate it in both directions. Rest. Compare your left leg and your right leg. Observe accurately the differences between both your legs. Then become aware of all the bones in your left leg.

Focus now on your right hip bone and the left one. Become aware of the two little joints which link your hip bones to your sacrum.

Focus now on your coccyx and move up to your sacrum. Feel how your sacrum is linked to the fifth lumbar vertebra. Move up the five lumbar vertebras one by one.

Continue to do this along all the twelve vertebra of your thorax. Expand your focus on to your rib cage. Feel each single rib and how each is connected to a vertebra at the back and to the sternum in the front. Focus on your sternum for a moment and then be aware of your entire rib cage. Feel your shoulder blades and your clavicles on both sides. Become simultaneously aware of the two shoulder joints and the big bones within your upper arms.

Shift your focus now to your elbows. Move along the two bones within your forearm until you come to your wrists. From here sense the five metacarpal bones of your palms. Feel the five little joints of each hand linking the fingers to the palm. Feel the three little bones within your finger, and the joints which link each of them up.

Focus again on the spine and become aware of your neck. From the seventh cervical vertebra slowly move one by one up to the first cervical vertebra. Become conscious of the spot where the base of your skull links to the first cervical vertebra. Feel your lower jaw and focus on the two jaw joints on the right and the left. Move your attention to the entire bony structure of your head.

All at once become aware of your whole skeleton. Now you have to physically do this last part of the exercise as a real movement and not in your imagination. Breathe in and contract all at once the muscles within your body as if you are compressing your bones. Hold this contraction as intensely as possible and for as long as you can. Then breathe out and relax. Repeat three times this form of contraction then rest for a while.

Exercise 2

Practicing this exercise will increase your ability to perceive and understand how your spine and organs are linked to each other. This kind of understanding is different from an intellectual insight that you will get when you study or analyze a human anatomy chart. It will greatly benefit you to look at such a chart before you start the exercises in this book. It will help you to get an impression of the shape and location of the organs in the body.

Through this exercise you will begin to explore the connections between your spine and the various organs. You will experience various physical feelings which will arise as a result of this encounter. You will also feel a wide range of sensations and occasionally you may also see different colors. The kinaesthetic impressions may or may not be pleasant and will differ according to the organs you focus on. All together you will attain a state of deep relaxation and will feel revitalised if all your organs are healthy and functioning properly. If you have problems with one or more of your organs you may experience an uncomfortable tension within the affected segment of your back. There may be various other sensations which differ for each individual. Some will feel a kind of tension, others a kind of burning, or a tickling sensation, and some may feel pain. However if there is any unusual sensation you are picking up then it should be observed closely.

For some of us this may reveal hidden organic problems probably at a very early stage and long before they show any obvious symptoms. If you practice this exercise several times and if you repeatedly notice discomfort and tension in a specific segment you should see the doctor. If he finds nothing then you are fortunate. You now have the chance to balance your body of light soon enough so that no physical problems will occur later. And if the doctor unfortunately finds something wrong in a specific organ you have identified then maybe it will save your life. A diagnosis at an early stage has always a greater chance of success-fully treating and curing a problem.

As this exercise is limited for people who are beginners in this kind of work the focus is limited to the main and solid organs and their interconnection to the spine. Once you get used to this practice and your self awareness has increased you can expand this journey through the rest of your body. You can reach and observe each place on your own. Some may reach the state of self awareness on a cellular level; others may reach deeper into their genetic level one day.

Take a position where you feel comfortable. Breathe deeply and feel the air moving through your nose into your body. Breathe out and feel the air leave your body the same way. Repeat this six times, breathing normally.

Become aware of the fact that your eyes are an entrance for light to enter your body. Collect as much light as you can with your eyes and move it inside your head to the brain. Now focus on your brain. Look at the brain as if you have turned your eyes backwards. Become aware of the two hemispheres of your brain and the cerebral divide that separates those two sides. Lead the light collected by your eyes deeper into the core of your brain. Now bring it down where the brain stem merges with the spinal cord.

Pass the cervical spine focusing now on each of its seven vertebra, one after the other. Lead the light down into the first three thoracic vertebrae. Hold your awareness between the third and the fourth vertebra for a while. Look for a connection from there to your lungs. Trust your first instinct even it is only a fleeting impression. It will become more stable as you continue to follow it. If you start questioning your first impressions your mind will take over and you will lose the thread of these delicate sensations. Become aware of your lungs, and bring it into your consciousness that they really exist. Focus for a little while on their function and how they supply your body with oxygen; pay tribute to your lungs for keeping you alive. Focus again on the lungs' connection to the spine and return to the spot between the third and the fourth thoracic vertebra.

Keep your awareness there then expand it down the thoracic vertebral cord until you are between the fifth and the sixth vertebra. Now look for a connection to your heart. Expand your awareness along this connection into your heart. Be conscious of the fact that you have a heart and honour this untiring little muscle no bigger than your fist. It is responsible for the flow of blood through your body. When it no longer beats your life will come to an end. Move back to the spine and expand again your awareness along the thoracic vertebra.

Between your ninth and your tenth thoracic vertebra pause for a moment and look for a connection to your liver. Expand your awareness into this big organ which is a kind of chemical factory within your body. Remain there for a while acknowledging the presence of your liver and the work it does to keep you alive. Slowly go back to the spine and move down the vertebra to the spinal cord. You may find it difficult to hold your awareness for a longer period. This will be a problem only in the beginning. Do not force yourself, keep it easy and learn to go with the flow. Your body is always there and all you have to do is become aware of the fact that your body is a living reality.

Expand your awareness along your spinal cord and stop between the 11th and 12th thoracic vertebra. Look for a connection to your spleen and move there. Your spleen has a vital role in keeping your immune system healthy. Dwell there for a moment then come back to the spine. Do not forget to remind yourself about the importance of each your organs. Be conscious that each one of them is an important part of your body. Now move back to the spine and once more down along the spinal cord.

Rest for a moment between the second and the third lumbar vertebra, where you will find a connection into your kidneys. Follow this path and expand your awareness until you reach the kidneys. Repeat what you did before, remain there, observing respectfully this pair of organs, and noting the specific feeling you are receiving. Then go back to the spine.

Now go down to the sacrum and focus your awareness there for a while. Observe your whole spinal cord from the sacrum to the brain. Observe all the neuronal connections between the spinal cord and the organs you have been to before. Include all these organs simultaneously in your observation. Hold this state for as long as it feels comfortable for you.

Exercise to Balance Life Energy along the Spine

We can find some common attributes when we compare life energy to water. Both are by nature permanently in motion. If water stagnates and there is no possibility of exchange with other bodies of water it will putrefy. Life energy within a human body has a similar characteristic. When it stagnates two different things can occur: in the first instance when the natural flow of life energy within the human body is hindered by a blockage it will lead to an increased heat which will manifest itself physically as an inflammatory state.

To see an example of how this affects our spine let us have a closer look at the inflammation of a nerve root. A number of reasons are responsible for the appearance of such a problem. What they have in common is that the tissue enclosing a nerve root becomes engorged. As a result of this the space around the nerve becomes narrowed and exerts pressure on its root at the spine. Then pain, numbness or tickling will occur within the extremities supported by the affected nerve. The original reasons for this nerve root compression are degenerative changes, prolapse, osteoporosis, tumours or infections such as borreliosis. All of these problems could be analyzed separately concerning to how they affect an imbalance in life energy, but for now we will limit our observation to the compressed nerve root.

Based on the fact that each physical structure possesses an electromagnetic equivalent we can simply say that the narrowing of tissue around a nerve root and the blood congestion there leads to a stagnation of life energy.

The second form of stagnation of life energy is comparable to a pond with little or hardly any exchange of its water. The result will be a muddy brew, an undrinkable and lifeless pool of water. This is similar to a muscle which is permanently under tension caused by certain destructive postures such as sitting in front of a computer for long periods of time. The muscles will develop hyperacidity and a lack of movement will additionally lead to a low metabolism. The reduced blood circulation does not allow an adequate supply of oxygen and the removal of toxins is reduced to a minimum. Tension and pain occur as a result of all this. When there is an area of stagnation in the physical body the level of life energy around such areas will be very low.

The shape of matter influences the electromagnetic field of an organism and the electromagnetic field provides the information which is necessary for the regeneration of matter at a cellular level. Therefore any kind of treatment to your back will be much more effective if supported simultaneously in the physical as well as in electromagnetic field of life energy. This will also be effective in preventing any kind of pathological degeneration when we start early enough to balance our body of light.

By practicing the following exercise you will learn to move life energy consciously within your body. It has a harmonizing and deeply relaxing effect and will in the long term avoid or dissolve all forms of stagnation of life energy. The focus on a number of spots along the spine increases the flow of life energy. This enlarges the space between your vertebra where the intervertebral discs are situated and builds up a kind of cushion of energy which protects vertebras and nerves.

Find a suitable position which is comfortable for you, either sitting upright on the edge of a chair or lying on your back. Place the tip of your tongue on your gum behind the two central upper front teeth. Breathe in and out consciously for a few times. Then focus your attention on a spot approximately an inch and a half, or three centimeters, behind your navel. Breathe in and out and continue to focus on this spot until you sense some sensation there. It may be a kind of tickling sensation or a feeling of warmth. If you find it difficult to feel anything, rub the spot gently with your fingertips on the surface of the skin. Then try again. Whatever sensation you pick up here, reinforce it by creating through your intentions a

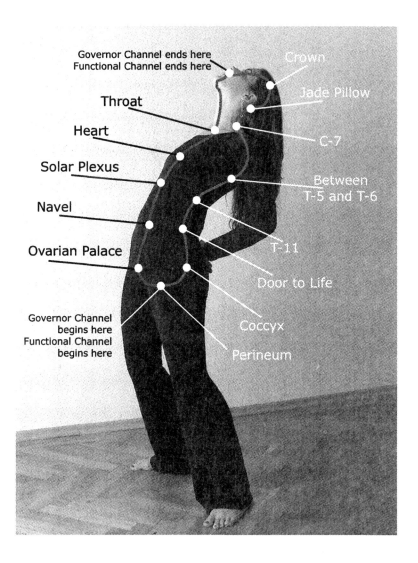

Governor Channel ends here
Functional Channel ends here

Crown

Throat

Jade Pillow

Heart

C-7

Solar Plexus

Between
T-5 and T-6

Navel

Ovarian Palace

T-11

Door to Life

Governor Channel
begins here
Functional Channel
begins here

Coccyx

Perineum

circular movement. If you are unable to do this at first, use your eyes to circle life energy at the navel point. Circle your eyes clockwise and then anti-clockwise keeping your focus on the navel point. Continue this until you can feel the sensation clearly and you have a distinct physical perception of how your Life energy moves in a circular motion around your navel point.

Now focus on a spot which is in middle of the upper edge of your pubic bone for a man and two fingers above if you are woman. Repeat the circular motion that you did at the navel point until you are able to perceive and rotate life energy in both directions.

Move your focus now to your perineum. Once again you look for any sensation here and reinforce it by circling life energy clockwise and anti-clockwise the way you had done before. After doing so bring your focus back to the point on your pubic bone and then once again back to the navel point. Once you have reached this spot you have completed the first stage of this exercise. As soon as you are familiar with these first three spots (navel point, pubic bone, perineum) you can move to the next point.

The next spot is approximately one inch (two centimetres) above the lower end of your coccyx. Focus on it and begin to move in a circular motion – first clockwise then anti-clockwise, noting any sensation you can feel there. Then move back point by point to the navel if you are doing this point for the first times. When you are ready to continue the exercises move your focus now up to the lumbar spine.

The next spot to focus on is situated between your second and your third lumbar vertebra. If you remember from the first part of the exercise this is the place where you can find a connection between your kidneys and your spine. Now focus with the aim of reinforcing the sensation you can perceive there. Whether you feel there warm or a tickling or any other sensations bring this into a circling clockwise and anti-clockwise movement. You circle there either with the support of your eyes or just with your intention as long as you are able to have a clear perception of your life energy rotating at this point. Once you have reached this stage move back slowly one point at a time until you arrive at your navel point where you first started with this exercise.

Begin the next part again by focusing on your navel point. With more practice you will find it easier to move the life energy in a circle as you move from one point to the next. Now find a spot between the 11th and the 12th thoracic vertebra. You will remember this spot as the initial point which increased your awareness of the link between your spleen and the spine. Once again as you had done before move the life energy in a circle in a clockwise and then in an anti-clockwise movement until you have build up a clear perception of this. Then move back point by point to your navel.

Now start again from the navel and move up point by point to a new spot on the spine. You will find it situated between the fifth and the sixth thoracic vertebra. This is where your heart is connected to your spine. Rotate gently the life energy with your intention in a clockwise and then anti-clockwise movement. Then move back point by point until you arrive once again at your navel.

As you continue to practice this exercise you will find a chaining of all the points from the navel to the seventh cervical vertebra. Repeat the technique of circling until you are successful in perceiving and moving consciously your life energy on this particular point. Then move step by step back to your navel point.

The next point in this cycle is the spot where your first cervical vertebra is linked to the base of your skull. Focus there and move your life energy in a clockwise and then anti-clockwise direction until you have the same sensation as you had in the other points before. Once you are at this stage you may find it much easier to activate all the points you have exercised on so far. You will be able to instantly create a circular movement by only breathing and focusing on these points.

The next step is to move is to move from the navel up to the very top of your skull. Focus there for a moment and initiate a circular movement of life energy first clockwise then anti-clockwise. After three weeks or so of daily practice you will be able to move the flow of life energy back to the navel on the front of your body.

Moving from the top of the skull, the first point on the way down is between your eyebrows just above the nose. Focus there for a moment and initiate a circular movement of life energy first clockwise then anti-clockwise.

The next point would be exactly the spot when you place your tongue on the inside of your gums and is directly below the nostrils. Focus there and circle the life energy until you can feel its movement clearly and precisely.

Now bring your focus to the top of your sternum between the ends of your clavicles and circle the life energy there in both directions. The next spot on the way down to the navel in the front of your body is situated in the centre of your sternum exactly in the middle of your nipples if you are a man. Keep your focus there and circle the life energy as you have done before. Then move down to the end of your sternum, the solar plexus. This is the last point to focus on and circle the life energy before you finally return to the navel point.

Once you are back at the navel from the front you have completed a full circle up your whole spine, first from the back, then from the front. Now you no longer need to complete the circle by moving back the way you came from as you are able to create a perpetual circular movement.

Move along this circle each day for as many times as you like and you will be delighted by its benefits. In time you will recognise that this exercise will balance you emotionally, help you to regenerate quickly and will literally recharge you when you are drained by all kinds of stress.

CHAPTER 6

Exercises for the Rebalancing of the Spine

How to Exercise

Have you ever given any thought to what happens within our body when we workout or do specific exercises? While exercising many of us tend to mechanically repeat a number of prescribed movements without being aware of what goes on in our system. This kind of unawareness reduces the benefit of exercising to a minimum because only a very small part of a whole person is involved. To achieve the optimal effect of an exercise it is necessary to be totally aware of any movement. This includes an accurate observation of all the details of how a specific movement feels. Is there any tension or strain felt in your limbs and which muscles and joints are involved? We also need to be conscious of how exercising a particular region of the body affects the rest of it. What changes can we observe when we practice a specific exercise over a period of time?

When we do an exercise for the first time we should do a detailed assessment of our present physical state in the beginning. This enables us to objectively recognise changes later when we compare the original state to the physical after repeating an exercise for a period of time. It will also increase our awareness of movement patterns which will enable to consciously avoid the ones which are destructive. We should not restrict our progress check to only our physical development but also closely observe our emotional state as well as our behavioural patterns. Taking into consideration that movement patterns are a result of work done by muscles, we should also keep in mind that the state of our muscles is an expression of our emotional state as well as our mental patterns. Exercising our muscles will not only make them stronger and more flexible but will also ease tension. Besides creating a stable change within our skeletal muscles we will also experience a change in our emotional and mental patterns.

Exercising will dissolve anxiety stored somewhere in the muscle tissues and this has an impact on the brain as well. When we change our movement patterns, we change the neuronal networks which are responsible for them. Our movement patterns are a result of our reaction to emotional states such as anxiety, and when we change the movement patterns then the original emotional state changes as well. When we apply the same mechanism to mental patterns such as defensiveness these can be changed when we work on our patterns of movement. In the long term we will see dramatic changes in our behaviour when we overcome destructive mental patterns on a physical level and regain the original state of our body.

Practicing exercises will have long lasting results if we consider it as an enjoyable and enriching experience rather than a bothersome duty that needs to be done. When we begin exercising we have made a conscious decision to take responsibility for our wellbeing and to get rid of whatever that is taking away our quality of life: back pain. This would mean that we will regain a lot of our personal freedom to start doing things for our well being instead of just reacting or giving in to circumstances.

Take *your* time. If you are able to spend about an hour daily exercising then do so. If this is not possible, two exercise sessions of twenty minutes each on a daily basis will be good. You can split the workouts into a morning and an evening unit. The morning unit should include exercises designed to increase your flexibility and the strength of your muscles. You will have a good start for your day when your muscles are warm and there is an increased blood flow within your joints. This enables you to effectively tackle your daily duties. The evening unit should focus more on relaxation and on increasing your self awareness. This will improve the quality of your sleep and give you deeper relaxation and as a result, increase your powers of regeneration. Your brain also has the opportunity to stabilize newly acquired patterns much better.

The perfect environment for a workout would be a place where you can be by yourself without any disturbance. Any distraction will make it more difficult for you. For this reason switch off your mobile phone, turn off your radio or your television. As far as possible do not allow anybody to interrupt you. This is your time! You should have a space that is large enough to enable you to lie and stretch your arms and legs freely. You should wear comfortable clothes while exercising and avoid anything that is too tight or hinders your movement. Eat only after exercising in the morning and begin your exercises in the evening at least one and a half hours after your dinner as you may have difficulties moving as well as practicing self awareness on a full stomach; it will be even better if you do these exercises just before you go to bed.

For some of these exercises you will need an empty wall where you can lean on. For some of the exercises you will also need a chair, a cube or you can use any stable box. Avoid working out on a plain wooden floor or even worse, a stone floor. This will be very uncomfortable and you may end up catching a chill. It is better to cover the floor with a carpet or any kind of gym mat. Occasionally you may need a flat cushion and a roll which you can put under your knees. From all the following exercises choose the ones which suit your present physical state. The detailed description will be a guideline for your choice of what is the best for the moment. There is certainly a difference for somebody who is suffering from severe pain or someone whose aim is to exercise for the prevention of back pain. From wherever you begin you have the opportunity to progress further. There is no need to do the exercises all at once.

Now that all the preconditions are met you can start to change your life by improving your present state of being free of pain and physical restrictions.

Lower Back Area

The lower back is defined as the part which begins at the first lumbar vertebra and continues down to the coccyx. It also includes the pelvis girdle and the hip joints. At the buttocks are the muscles which enable us to straighten our hips and help to keep the trunk erect. The function of the muscles along the front of the upper leg is to bend our hips. Involved in this movement of bending the whole trunk forward are the psoas muscles. Along either side of the spine we can find the autochthon muscles which are responsible for keeping the spine erect and also to support the upright posture. The stomach muscles are responsible for our ability to bend and to twist the trunk. They are also important in providing additional support to the autochthon muscles along the spine by holding the trunk in an upright position.

Exercises for the Lower Back Area

Assessing your Present Physical State

Stand upright and bend forward as far as you can to reach your toes. Observe closely how flexible you are and record any restriction you feel with this movement. If you experience any pain do not go any further, try to locate it as accurately as you can and record it. If you feel some tickling or numb like sensations radiating in your legs locate and record them as well.

Now rotate your trunk to the right and to the left. Check again how flexible you are when you do this movement. If you experience any pain then record your observations as well.

Lie flat on the floor with your arms along the sides of your body. Bend your knees and move your heels closer to your buttocks until you find a comfortable position. Keeping your pelvis in contact with the floor begin to circle your sacrum.

Circle in both directions, clockwise and anticlockwise. While doing so focus first on your coccyx. Begin with very small circles and then slowly increase the radius until you reach your limit. Observe closely if you are really making a circular movement with your sacrum or if it had become more elliptic. Are you equally flexible in both directions or are you flexible in one direction rather than the other.

Still lying on the floor continue circling your sacrum without lifting your pelvis and focus now on your genitals. Make the same observations as before – watch if you are equally flexible on both sides and whether you are making circular or elliptical movements?

Continue to circle your sacrum on the floor focusing now on your navel. Check again to see if you are doing circles and if you can feel a difference between the clockwise and anticlockwise movement.

Now stop and rest a little then record your observations. This assessment should be done once a week as long as you are exercising. It will give you an objective feedback of your progress.

The perfect time to practice the following exercises is in the morning before breakfast. During the night when you sleep there are only very few movements within your lower back. As a result of this the muscles tighten up and in the morning you will experience this as stiffness. To warm up the muscles, increase the blood flow within them and to become more flexible you should exercises at this time. The advantage is that you will have fewer problems with your back during the day.

Exercise 1 Stretching the Lower Dorsal Extensors:

This exercise should be done if you have problems bending forward and if you cannot do a proper circle with your sacrum.

Lie on your back with arms by your sides. Bend your knees and put your feet flat on the floor. Clasp your arms around and just under both knees. If you are not flexible enough you can start by holding the back of your thighs. Later as your flexibility increases you can grasp with your hands the back of your upper legs directly under your knees.

Bring your head and shoulders forward to your knees and gently sway forward and backward on your lower back.

Exercise 2 for Distension of the Lower Dorsal Extensors:
If you experience pain and strain in your neck while being in the position described above then it is better to start with this exercise first.

Sit on the edge of a chair and put your feet a little apart on a box in front of you. Bend your trunk forward, cross your fingers and stretch your arms forward.

Breathe in and as you breathe out pull your arms from the elbows down keeping your forearms still reaching to the front of you. Relax when breathing in again. Repeat this movements several times.

Exercise 1: Stretching of the Lower Back Extensors and the Buttock Muscles
This exercise should be done if you have problems bending forward and if you cannot perform a proper circle with your sacrum.

Lie on your back, bend your knees and put your feet flat on the floor and relax your arms along the sides of your body. Clasp your hands around your right knee and pull it gently against the chest while breathing out.

Now lower the right knee and extend it straight on the floor. Shake your leg to relax the muscle.

Repeat all of this with your left leg.

Exercise 2: Stretching of the Lower Back Extensors and the Buttock Muscles

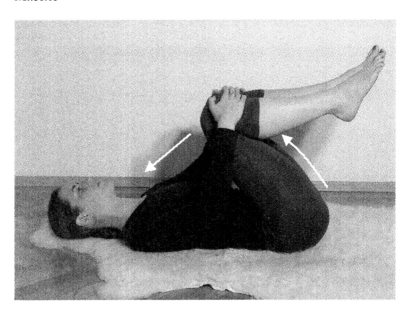

This exercise should be done if you have problems bending forward and if you cannot do a proper circle with your sacrum.

Lie on your back bend your knees and put your feet flat on the floor and your arms along the sides of your body. Clasp your hands around your knees and pull them gently against the chest.

Hold this position for as long as it is possible working up to a maximum of 25 seconds. As you breathe out go back to starting position.

Exercise 3: Stretching of the Lower Back Extensors and the Buttock Muscles

This exercise should be done if you have problems bending forward and if you cannot do a proper circle with your sacrum.

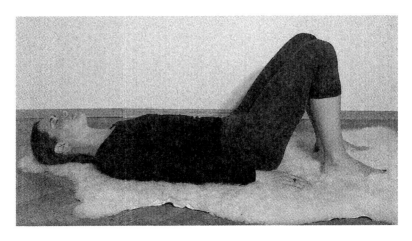

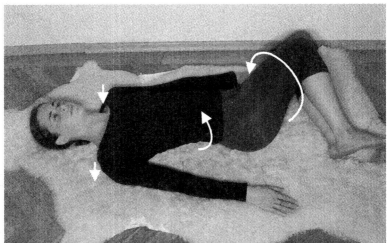

Lie on your back, bend your knees and put your feet flat on the floor and relax your arms along your body.

Put your knees together and drop them both as far as possible to the right. Keep both your shoulders in contact with the ground. As you move your knees to the right your hips and buttocks will rise from the floor.

Move back to the starting position. Now do the same

movement and drop your knees to the left. Repeat this exercise several times on either side.

Exercise 4: Stretching of the Lower Back Extensors and the Buttock Muscles
This exercise should be done if you have problems bending forward and if you cannot do a proper circle with your sacrum.

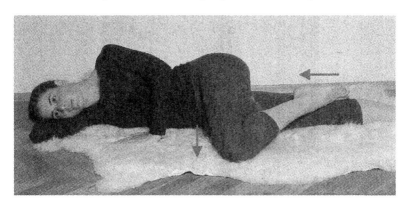

Lie on your right side with your right leg stretched. Bend your left knee and pull your left leg up towards your upper body so that your left foot touches your right knee.

Bring your left knee across your right leg and touch the floor.

Raise your left knee up while keeping the left foot on the right knee. Turn to your left side and repeat all these movements with your right leg.

Exercise 5: Stretching of the Lower Back Extensors and the Buttock Muscles
This exercise should be done if you have problems bending forward and if you cannot do a proper circle with your sacrum.

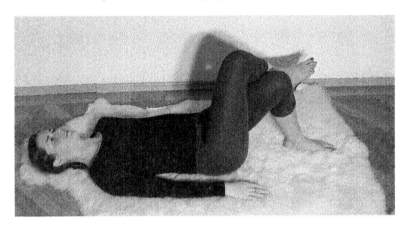

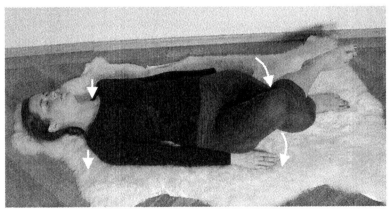

Lie on your back with your arms relaxed along the body. Bend your knees and put your feet flat on the floor.

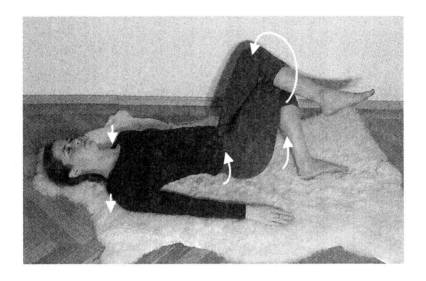

Cross your left leg over your right leg and bring your knees to the right side towards the floor as far as possible. Raise your knees and repeat this exercise up to six times.

Then cross your right leg over your left one and bring your knees to the left side towards the floor as far as you are able to. Raise your knees and repeat this up to six times.

Exercise for Stretching the deep buttock muscles:
This exercise should be done if you have problems bending forward and if you cannot do a proper circle with your sacrum.

Sit on the floor and extend your right leg. Cross the left leg over the right and bend the left knee placing the left foot flat on the floor. Put your left hand on the floor and rest your right hand on the left leg.

Now pull the left knee towards the right hip as far as possible and hold this position for as long as you can. Now repeat this exercise on the other side.

Stretching the hip benders and knee extensors

Stand close to a wall and place your left palm on the wall. With your right hand pull up your lower right leg to the back.

As your knee stretches contract your upper leg muscles against the movement of the knee. Relax. Repeat several times with the right leg than continue with the left.

Stretching of the back muscles of the lower leg

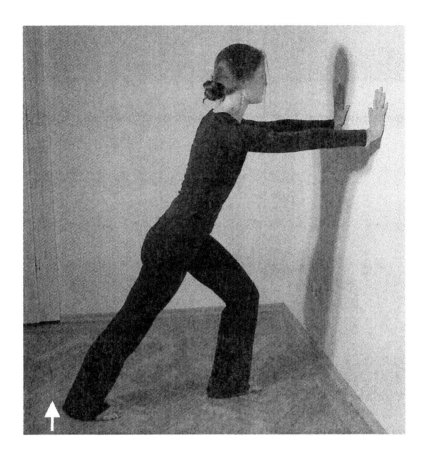

Place both of your hands on the wall. Move your right leg one step behind your left. Lift your right heel several times and then continue by placing your left leg one step behind your right and lifting your left heel.

Stretching of the Abductors

Sit on the edge of a chair and place your right leg as far back as possible and as far away from your left leg. Press the inner part of your right foot towards the floor. Relax.

Repeat all this with your left leg.

Strengthening Exercises

Increasing the strength of the muscles in your buttocks will help if you experience difficulties in straightening your trunk after bending forward. Your abdominal muscles give the lumbar area of your spine more stability as they release the autochthon muscles along the spine. If you have problems twisting your trunk you have a good reason for strengthening your abdominal muscles.

Exercise Strengthening of the Buttock Muscles

Lie flat on the floor with your arms by the sides of your body. Rest your heels on a small box. Tense your buttocks and simultaneously lift your pelvis and the lumbar region. Repeat this several times.

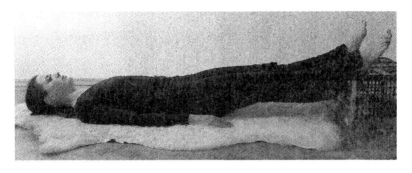

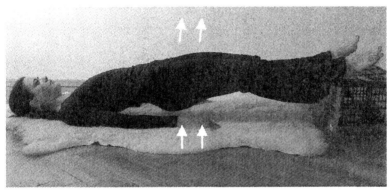

Exercise 1: Strengthening of the Abdominal Muscles

Lie flat on the floor with your arms by the sides of your body.

Bend your knees and put your feet on the floor. Lift your pelvis as far as you can towards the ceiling. Repeat this several times.

Exercise 2: Strengthening of the Abdominal Muscles

Lie flat on the floor. Bend your knees and lift your feet parallel to the floor.

Push your knees towards the ceiling while lifting your pelvis a little.

Exercise 3: Strengthening of the Abdominal Muscles

Lie flat on the floor with your arms by the sides of your body. Bend your knees and put your heels on the floor, lift your toes.

Turn your arms slightly inward, pull your palms up and push

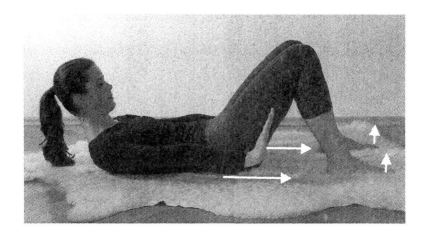

your hands against your feet. Lift your head and shoulders up as far as possible.

Exercise 4: Strengthening of the Abdominal Muscles

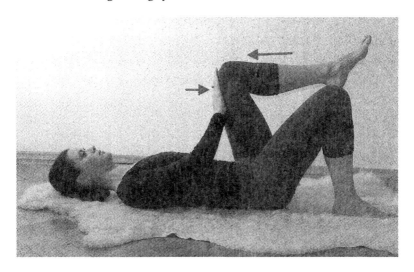

Lie flat on the floor. Bend your knees. Lift the right knee and push it against the resistance of your left hand. Repeat this with the left knee and the right hand.

Exercise 5: to Strengthen the Abdominal Muscles

Lie flat on the floor. Bend your knees, then lift them both and push them together against the resistance of your hands.

Combined Exercises for the Lumbar Area

The following two exercises cover the whole lumbar vertebra. The first one is to increase the flexibility there and the second is to increase strength and stability.

Cat Stretch

Get down on the floor on all fours keeping your back flat and distributing your weight equally on all sides.

Slide your hands forward and bend your elbows so that they touch the floor.

Lower your head to the floor and raise your buttocks up.

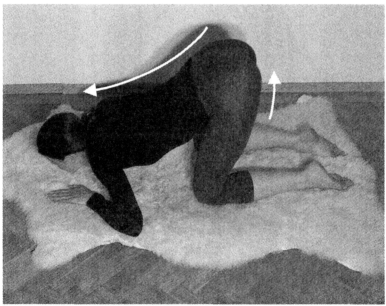

Move gently back so that your stomach touches your upper leg and you are almost sitting on your ankles with your buttocks close to your heels.

Go back to the starting position.

Bring your chin to your chest and pull in your abdominals as you arch your back like a cat.

Relax your abdominal muscles and smoothly raise your head to the starting position.

Tree Stand

This exercise is perfect in creating strength and stability for the whole lower back area. The Tree Stand is not only highly effective in training all the muscles there; it is also a way of build up a belt of life energy around you. This is perfect for preventing lower back problems on the one hand and on the other the regular practice of this exercise will additionally provide you with emotional stability and grounding.

The exercise is to be learned in three steps each building upon the other. Once you have had some practice it will take you only a few minutes every day to benefit greatly from this exercise.

Step One

Lean against a wall and stand with your legs shoulder width apart. Bend your knees as closely as you can to a 90 degree position.

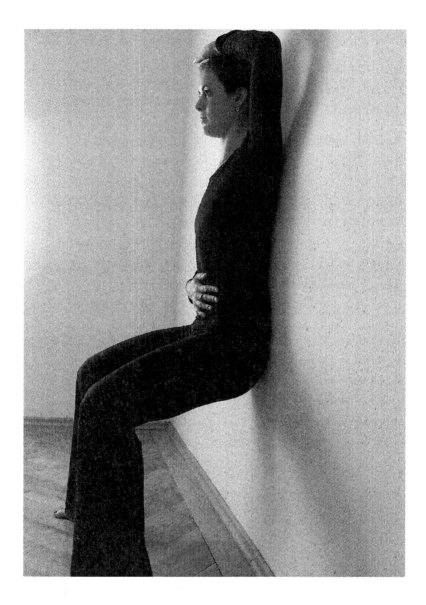

Now press your whole spine from the sacrum to the base of your head as closely as possible against the wall. Bring your chin near to the chest and straighten the whole spine so that there is no more space between the wall and your spine.

Holding this position, breathe in deeply lifting your diaphragm up and expanding your stomach. Breathe out and lower your diaphragm and pull in your stomach. Repeat this up to twenty times.

Step Two

Stand with your feet shoulder width apart and ensure that

your weight is equally distributed on both your feet. Be aware that your weight is also equal on the soles of your feet. Your heels, toes, the forefeet and the arches have equal pressure on the floor.

Bend the knees so that they are in line with your toes. Move your pelvis a little forward and bring your chin to your chest to straighten and stretch all your vertebrae. Imagine a string running straight from the top of your head right through your body down to the perineum and from there to the floor. Align your standing position along this imaginary string without building up any tension.

Keeping the shoulders and neck relaxed bend your elbows and lift your arms. Hold your thumbs upright and look forward between your thumbs and your forefingers. Holding this position for a while and check if your spine is still straight and there is no build up of tension anywhere within your body.

Step Three

You will become familiar with this position after a couple of days of practicing the Tree Stand described in Step Two. You can now focus on your breathing. The first type of breathing you combine with this Tree Stand posture is the same as the one you have done in step one. Breathe in deeply so that your diaphragm lifts up and your stomach expands. Breathe out and lower your diaphragm so that you pull in the stomach. Repeat this up to twelve times.

Now as you breathe in sharply contract your anus at the same time. With your breath you focus on the navel point, one inch behind your navel. Circle whatever sensation is felt there four times in each direction. Now breathe out relax and repeat this breathing several times.

Neck and Shoulder Area

It can be broadly said that the neck and shoulder areas are those parts of our body which are covered by the *trapezius* muscle. This includes the cervical and thoracic vertebra. The *trapezius* muscle is divided in three parts, one covers the neck, another covers the shoulder blades and a third part the back of the chest down to the 12th thoracic vertebra.

Along the cervical vertebra we can find a first layer of autochthon muscles and above the *sternocleidomastoideus* and the descending part of the *trapezius* muscle. All of them are responsible for our ability to bend our heads, to straighten it up, to turn it from side to side and as well as to rotate it. Another important group of muscles connected to the *hyoid* bone is important for our ability to make these kinds of movements with our head.

Exercises for the Neck and Shoulder Area

The two exercises described below are very complex but effective in solving and preventing neck and shoulder problems. They should be practised daily if you have neck and shoulder problems; for prevention it is enough to do the exercises twice a week. Both exercises should be done with great self awareness so you can get maximum benefit from them. When you start practicing the exercises it is useful for you to read aloud and record the description on a tape. You can then easily follow the instructions when you hear them instead of interrupting the exercise to read what is coming next.

Exercise 1

Lie on your back close your eyes and be aware of how your body touches the floor. Feel how far the distance is between the floor and your lumbar spine.

Then focus on the distance between your neck and the floor. Use your fingers to check if your feelings correlate to the actual distance. Check whether this distance is equal on both sides the right and the left. Put your hands on the floor with the arms along the sides of your body. Is there a difference between the right and left shoulder when you check its contact to the floor?

Now check the contact of your buttocks to the floor and do they feel equal? Focus on your wrists now. Is there any space between them and the floor? If there is some space is it the same on the right and the left side?

Check your knees and your calves and their contact the floor. Are your hands lying equally on the floor?

Are you breathing through both nostrils in the same way? Are your lungs expanding equally on both sides as you breathe in? Can you feel your breathing within your shoulders?

Now focus on your head. Does the nose point straight up? Are you looking straight at the ceiling?

Close your eyes. Turn your head to the left, then to the right and check if your flexibility in these movements is equal on both sides. If you experience more restriction on one side as you turn then look at your shoulders, at your spine and your whole back. Check whether you can find any kind of sensation somewhere in these areas. Turn from side to side for 25 times then stop and rest for a moment.

Push your hands towards your feet without lifting them off the floor, and at the same time push your shoulders down towards your feet as you stretch your neck. Relax.

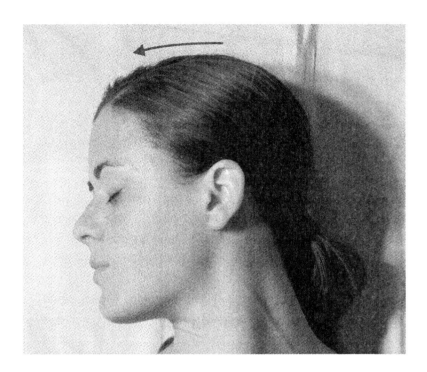

Then turn your head to the right and push your left shoulder towards your feet and pull your right shoulder up.

Turn your head to the left and simultaneously push your right shoulder down and pull your left shoulder up. Repeat these movements for as long as your shoulders move automatically when you turn your head. Then stop and rest.

Place one hand over the other close to and below your navel point. Now turn your head from right to left and back again. Lift your shoulders a little as you do this movement so that your left shoulder and the upper part of your back is off the floor as you turn your head to the right.

When you turn to the left lift your right shoulder and the upper part of your back off the floor once again. Repeat this

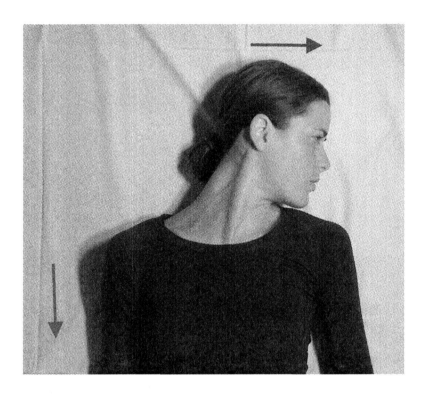

for 25 times so as to loosen your upper back as much as possible. Stop.

Next cross your arms over your chest and clasp the left shoulder with your right hand and the right shoulder with your left. Once again turn your head from one side to the other and observe if the range of the movement has increased. Stop and rest.

Place your arms alongside your body and turn your head again from one side to the other. Coordinate this head movement with the movements of your eyes; as you turn right look as far as possible over the right corner of your eyes and over the left corner as you turn your head to the left.

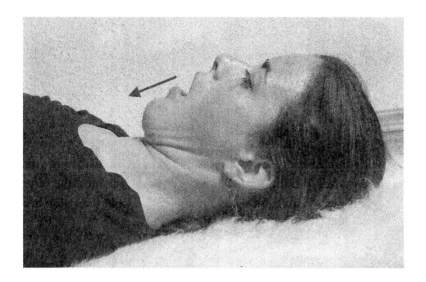

Repeat this movement for a while and observe whether the flexibility of your movement increases. Continue to do this eye movement as you turn your head but now press your tongue against the right cheek when you turn your head to the right and to the left cheek when you turn your head to the left. Observe if this improves the ease of your movement. Stop.

Keep your eyes focused on a point in the ceiling and turn your head from left to right and back. Repeat this for a number of times. Stop.

Turn your head from one side to the other without doing anything else. Stop. Now move your chin as close as possible to your chest without lifting your head off the floor. You can open your mouth and push your lower jaw so that it is closer to the chest: Hold the stretch along your spine for as long as you can then relax and rest.

Lay on your back with the arms along the sides of your body. Close your eyes and visualize turning your head from side to side. Your visualization should be so intense that you feel the movements kinaesthetically as if you are actually doing it. It may happen that you will experience some minimal muscular movement and if this occurs take it as a good sign that you are doing very well.

Continue now to visualize the stretch in your neck as you push your shoulders towards your feet. Then visualize turning your head while pulling one shoulder up and t pushing the other one down. Visualize this as vividly as possible then stop and rest.

This time do the actual movement one more time. Turn your head from one side to the other. Then move your chin as closely as possible to your chest and hold the tension within your spine for as long as possible. Stop and rest for a while.

Observe if you can recognise any changes from the very beginning of this exercise. Check all the parts of your body again as you have done before: your neck, lumbar spine, shoulders and buttocks.

Exercise 2

Lay on your back the arms along your body and observe your shoulders. Are your shoulders touching the floor symmetrically? If not then check how far up they are. Try to identify the muscles which are so tensed that they hinder your shoulders from touching the floor completely. Check how your entire back touches the floor. Use your hand to find out how much space there is between your lumbar vertebra and the floor.

Then close your eyes and relax as much as possible for a while.

Now lift your arms to 90 degrees up and bend your elbows. Clasp the outer part of your left elbow with your right hand and with your left hand clasp your right elbow on the inside. Push your right elbow as far as possible towards the floor.

Now change direction and push your left elbow as far as possible towards the floor. Repeat these movements up to 25 times.

Next as you continue to move your elbows from one side to the other turn your head as far as possible to the left as you push the left elbow to the Then turn your head to the right as you push your right elbow close to the floor. Stop and rest with your arms by the side of your body.

Bring your arms to the same position as before and simultaneously move your elbows and head a few times in the same direction.

Then move your head in the opposite direction – turn it to the left when you push your right elbow down and to the right when you push your left elbow towards the floor. Repeat this 25 times. Stop and rest.

Focus on a point on the ceiling while pushing your elbows towards the floor from one side to the other as you turn your head in the same direction. Do this for 25 times. Then continue the same movements 25 times more without focusing on the ceiling. Stop and rest with your arms along your body.

Stretch your arms up to the ceiling and interlock the fingers of both hands. Lock your elbows while moving your arms to the right side bend your right wrist and bring the back of your right hand as close as possible to the floor.

Do the same movement now to your left. As you do this you

will feel a stretch between your shoulder blades. Repeat these movements 25 times than stop and rest.

Once again stretch your arms towards the ceiling and place your palms together in a prayer position. As you gently rock your shoulders from left to right and back ensure that your palms do not move against each other. Continue to do this movement so that your arms and fingertips get closer and closer towards the floor.

Lift your shoulders and twist your whole trunk as you expand this movement but ensure that your sacrum and your hips always stay on the floor. Repeat these movements 25 times then stop and rest with your arms lying symmetrically along your body.

Stretch your arms parallel to each other 90 degree up to the

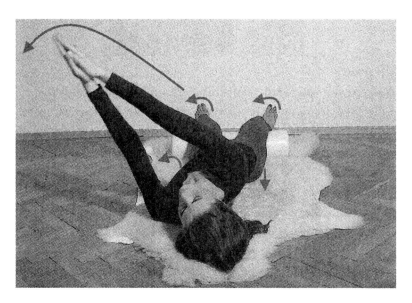

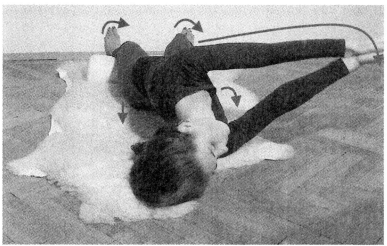

ceiling. Bend your wrists and as you do so lift both your shoulder blades both off the floor. Repeat this movement a number of times. Then bend your right wrist and lift the right shoulder blade. And as bend your left wrist lift your left shoulder.

After a number of repetitions bend both your wrists and together lift both your right and left shoulder blades off the floor. Stop and rest with your arms along the body.

Place your palms on your breast muscles with your elbows resting on the floor. Without lifting the palms from the breast lift your elbows up as much as possible and let them sink to

the floor again. Repeat this 25 times then rest with the palms still on your breast muscles. After a while do another 25 repetitions of these movements then rest again.

Lift your elbows up to shoulder height and make small circles in a clockwise direction. Slowly increase the radius as far as

possible without lifting the palms from the breast. Then repeat the same movement anticlockwise. Stop and rest with your palms on your breast muscles.

Now visualize the same clockwise and anticlockwise movements. Your visualisation has to be so strong that you really can feel the movements within your arms without doing them. Stop and rest a little.

Next lift again your elbows as far as possible towards the ceiling a number of times. Then push your elbows first towards your feet and then pull them up to your ears. Repeat this 25 times then rest with your arms along your body.

Move your arms straight behind your head until the back of your hands touches the floor. Bring them back to the starting position. Repeat this movement a number of times.

Stop when your arms in a position where they are pointing upright at 90 degrees and bring your thumbs together. Circle now with both arms in a clockwise direction and widen these circles as far as it is possible for you. Repeat it now in an anti-clockwise direction.

Now circle with only one arm first clockwise then anti-clockwise beginning with a very small radius and expanding this until you reach your limit.

Repeat this with the other arm then stop and rest with both your arms along your body.

Push one shoulder after the other down towards your feet so that you hands move towards your knees and then pull them up again so that your shoulders are now closer to your ears.

Repeat the same movements with your hands resting on your hips and do 25 repetitions in each position.

Now do the same movement as if you are doing a back stroke in the water. Stretch one arm behind your head and push the other one towards your feet. Repeat this 25 times. Stop and rest.

Lift your arms again to 90 degrees up and bend your elbows.

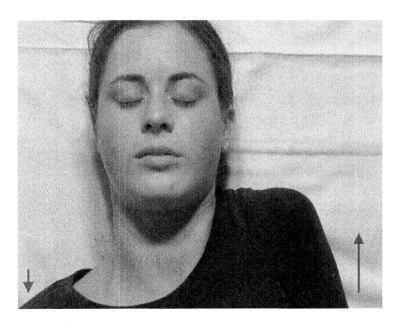

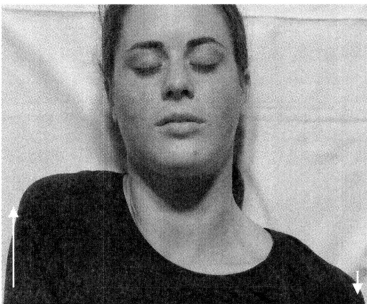

Clasp with your right hand the outside of your left elbow and
with your left hand the inside of your right elbow. Holding this

position push your arms behind your head towards the floor and then move they back to your chest again. Repeat this for 25 times then rest.

Stretch your arms up to the ceiling and interlock the fingers of both hands. Lock your elbows while moving your arms to the right side bend your right wrist and bring the back of your

right hand as close as possible to the floor.

Do the same movement now to your left. As you do this you will feel a stretch between your shoulder blades. Repeat these movements 25 times then stop and rest.

Check if you recognise how differently your shoulders feel on the floor now. Is there any difference about how your whole back feels now? How do you feel all in all? Observe closely any changes you noticed from the beginning of this exercises and every time when you practice it.

Body Exercises for the Whole Spine

When the spine becomes increasingly flexible it helps prevents back pain and also enables us to discover some of our hidden potentials. Any restriction in movement which affect our back will always be manifested on a physical, mental or an emotional level in some form or other. The restricted flexibility of our spine can be both: the cause as well as the outcome of a disturbance of the flow of life energy within our body. It will then lead to a low standard of life quality and a lack of perception of life energy through our own sensual organs.

The following two exercises are designed to increase the flexibility of our spine with the aim of opening it up for a more intense flow of life Energy. Besides preventing spine problems physically, the regular practice of these exercises promises to stabilize the emotional life and leads to an open and flexible mind. The exercises will create some changes within our brain function which will increase our self perception and enable us to perceive life energy through our sense organs as we were used to doing when we were small children. All in all these exercises bring us closer to a state of a well balanced self which will change our understanding of life as we become conscious about being a part of it instead of feeling separated of it. Practicing these exercises will also reenergize those parts of our body which are lacking life energy. It will make you feel better, more vitalized and attractive to others because of an increased and balanced vibrancy that you transmit.

Exercise 1 – Snake Movement
This exercise imitates the movement of a snake. Often we tend to have a wrong concept of how a snake really moves. When you ask people to show you the movement of a snake with their arm most of them will show it by sliding their arms up and down, while others will move their arms from one side to the other. If a snake were to move like this it would not be able to go anywhere. It is a combination of a vertical and a horizontal movement which makes a snake glide. Basically we do the same with our vertebra – we simultaneously move them up and down and also sideways against each other.

Snake Movement – Variation 1

Lie on your back with your arms lying alongside the body and bend your knees so that the soles of your feet are touching the floor. Breathe in and lift your pelvis. While breathing out slide your lumbar vertebrae against each other to the left and to the right one by one. Try to do the movement gently to ensure that each one of your vertebra moves as much as possible. For some people this may be very difficult but with a little practice you will be able to increase your flexibility to a point where this sliding movement will become easy and enjoyable.

Now breathe in and lift the lower end of your chest. As you breathe out continue to slide the thoracic vertebrae against each other one by one. This will be more difficult as the thoracic vertebrae are not that flexible because they are a part of the rib cage. However it is possible to slide them against

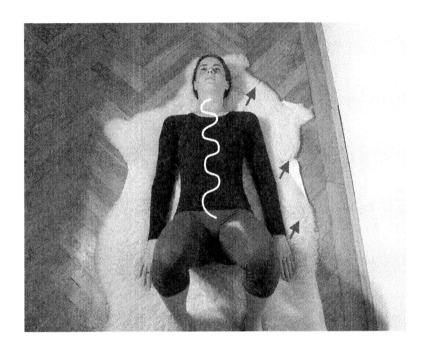

each other in small, gentle movements. Be really conscious of the movement of each single vertebra not just a few of them together.

Once again breathe in and lift your head a little. Continue the

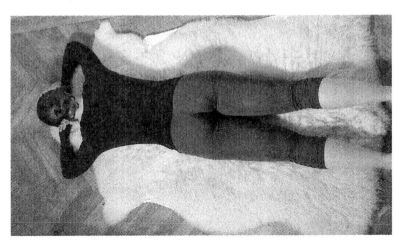

sliding movement along your cervical vertebra.

Start again by breathing in as you lift your pelvis and repeat the whole movement until you can feel a warm sensation on your forehead. This is a sure sign that you are doing the right thing as all your energy channels along your spine have opened up.

Snake Movement – Variation 2

Lay on your stomach rest your forehead on the back of your hands. Lift your pelvis as you breathe in and while breathing out slide your lumbar vertebrae one by one gently against each other from side to side.

Breathe in and lift the lower end of your chest. As you breathe out slide your thoracic vertebrae against each other one by one from side to side.

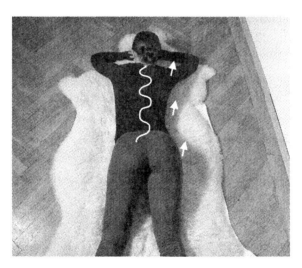

Now lift your head a little while breathing in and slide your cervical vertebrae against each other while breathing out. Breathe in and lift your pelvis again and repeat the whole snake movement as described above again and again until you experience a warm sensation or heat on your forehead.

Exercise 2 – Energizing the Brain
This exercise is designed to activate and balance your spine and your brain. As your spine increases in flexibility you will begin to feel more energized and alive. These are not the only benefits you will gain by practicing this exercise regularly at least once a week. One main advantage is that your brains will literally grow by creating new neuronal clusters on the cerebral cortex. As a result of this your self awareness will increase and you will have an altered perception of life energy on other humans as well as animals and plants.

Lie on your back, close your eyes and be aware of how your body touches the floor. Place your hands on the floor, with your arms along the sides of your body. Turn your head to the left then to the right and back again. To increase the range of your turning movement look as far as possible over the right corner of your eyes when you turn right and over the left corner when you turn to the left.

Repeat this for a while and observe whether the range of your movements increases. Continue to do this eye movement as you turn your head but now press your tongue against the right cheek when you turn your head to the right and to the left cheek when you turn your head to the left. Observe if this again improves the ease of your movement. Stop.

Keep your eyes focused on a point in the ceiling and turn your head from left to right and back. Repeat this for a number of times. Stop. Turn your head from one side to the other without doing anything else. Stop.

Now move your chin as close as possible to your chest without lifting your head off the floor. You can open your mouth and push your lower jaw so that it is closer to the chest: Hold the stretch along your spine for as long as you can then relax and rest.

Now stretch your legs with your coccyx make a few circles first to the right then to the left. Bend your knees so that the soles of your feet touch the floor and circle your coccyx once again in both directions. While doing this put focus mentally on your sexual organs. Continue to do the circles but now focus mentally on your navel point. Stop and relax.

Start again to circle your coccyx on the floor and at the same time circle your upper back and the back of your head keeping both of them on the floor as well. Circle for some times clockwise then circle anti-clockwise. As you continue to circle focus simultaneously on your sexual organs, your navel and the front of your chest. Circle a number of times in each direction then stop and rest.

Stretch your legs and rock your whole body for a while starting from the heels up to your head so that your chin moves to the chest and then moves back up again. Stop and rest.

Now with your legs still stretched out circle your pelvis slowly on the floor as if you are following an imaginary clockface. Move from twelve to one, to two and so on. At the same time you circle the back of your head in an anti-clockwise direction, from twelve to eleven, to ten and so on.

Stop for a moment and bend your knees so that your soles touch the floor. Continue to circle but change directions now so that your pelvis moves anti-clockwise and the back of your

head in a clockwise direction. Stop and rest.

Now imagine all these movements: the circling of the pelvis and the head in opposite directions. Imagine these as intensely as possible so that you can feel these movements within your body as if you are really doing them. Stop and rest.

Sit up now and put your soles on the floor and your hands by your side. As you circle your pelvis horizontally on the floor in a clockwise direction circle your head vertically in an anti-clockwise direction. Then change directions once again and circle your pelvis vertically in an anti-clockwise direction and your head horizontally in a clockwise direction.

Change again and circle your pelvis horizontally and your head vertically but this time do both in clockwise direction first

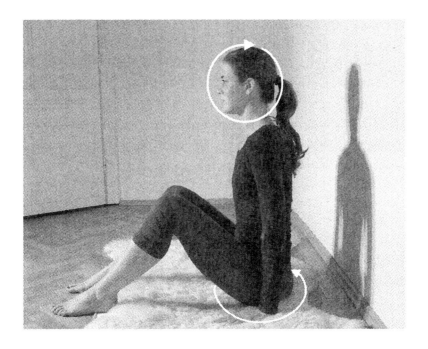

then anti-clockwise. Change once more and this time circle your pelvis horizontally anticlockwise and your head vertically in a clockwise direction and then do the reverse. Stop and rest.

Still in a sitting position stretch your legs and without any pressure put your hands behind your body on the floor. Starting from the pelvis rock your whole body now moving your stomach towards the ceiling while rocking up and drawing in your stomach when rocking down. Stop.

Do some quick circles with your head and pelvis in the two directions then stop. Lie down on your back and rest.

Move your chin as close as possible to your chest without lifting your head from the floor. You can open your mouth and push your lower jaw down to so that it comes closer to the chest, while keeping the stretch within your spine as long as you can repeat this a few times times. Then stop and rest.

As you turn your head from one side to the other push the right shoulder towards your knees and pull your left shoulder up to the ear and do the reverse when you turn to the left. Now put your hands on your chest and continue to move your shoulders down to the right and left while turning your head from side to side. Stop and rest.

Sit up and turn your head from one side to the other while you look as far as possible over the right corner of your eyes when turning right and to the left when turning left. Bend your head up and down for a couple of times. Continue bending your head but move your eyes in the opposite direction, look up when you bend your head down and look down when you move your head up. Then change directions and move your eyes and your head in the same direction.

Lastly bend your head up and down without controlling your eye movements. Do some quick circles with your head, vertically and horizontally, clockwise and anti-clockwise. Stop, lie on your back and rest.

Bend your knees and circle your pelvis and the back of your head gently, first clockwise then anti-clockwise. Stop.

Gently turn your head from left to right and back again focusing mentally on your chin first. As you continue turning your head focus now on your mouth then on the tip of your nose, your eyes, your eyebrows, and your forehead and up to the top of your head. One at a time do this movement till you reach the top of your skull. Stop.

Massage your scalp with your fingers. Then breathe into your brain and bring all your awareness there for a while.

Stop and rest. Observe carefully to see if there are any changes from your toes to the top of your head. Check if there is any difference in the way you perceive yourself compared to your perception before you started this exercise.

PART THREE

How to Help Others

CHAPTER 7

Directed Care – The Therapeutic Touch

Hands on Healing - The Most Ancient Method of Treatment

What is a mother's first instinctive reaction when she finds her child suffering from any kind of pain? She will automatically touch her child, placing her hands on any area of discomfort. She will place her hands on the baby's abdomen to soothe the baby when it is suffering from intestinal cramps. When she holds her baby in the arms close to her own body, it is as if by this intense touch she is drawing her child within herself to sort out any problems and comfort her baby.

We often touch painful areas on our own body with the aim of easing the pain. Some of us have experienced being touched and comforted by someone else who has managed to get rid of the pain or had at least bring it down to a more tolerable level. This is what humans – and other mammals – have done from the very beginning of their existence. Touching someone to ease their suffering was probably the beginning of every kind of medical treatment. Touching someone with the aim of helping is more than mere medical treatment. A person with the intention to help will unify with the one who is receiving healing. Through this act of healing, the healer becomes a manifestation of the universal power of love.

The instinctive reaction of a mother as well as the intentional act of a healer relieves not only physical pain, it also provides an emotional relief. Even the simple act of hugging somebody as a form of comfort is an act of healing. It is worth looking closely at this simple form of touch in every aspect because it affects one's physical and emotional states. Without a doubt, any form of touch has an impact on the brain. After being touched by someone who has the intention to help, one may experience less pain or in the best cases, no pain at all. This leads us to the question as to how the brain knows which kind of stimulus of nerve endings within our skin creates a healing impact, and which is a coincidental touch or something else. Touching someone on the surface of the body will lead to some form of information transfer. The brain transforms these stimuli of touch into a self healing process. The touch includes a physical, emotional and mental aspect and the brain knows exactly where the intentional touch is addressed, either physically, emotionally or both. Life energy, or chi, has the ability to carry all these types of information, as mentioned earlier in chapter four. As soon as someone places their hands on somebody else with the intention to help or to heal there will be an exchange of life energy between them.

Such an exchange of life energy takes place between all living creatures. Every time we interact with somebody there is an exchange of life energy, either as an individual or as a group. This kind of invisible interaction explains why we feel better in the presence of some people or worse with some others. The point is, if such a phenomenon exists then it can be consciously used for healing – not only by "gifted" individuals but by anyone who would like to do healing work. There is a wide range of possibilities as to how this can be done.

A number of different hands on healing techniques exist. Some are designed to have a more general impact on a person, while others are more sophisticated and enable the healer to work directly on a specific problem. If we want to use hands on healing therapy successfully for spine and back problems we have to take into consideration that a change on a physical level needs to be created. Such an approach differs from other techniques which can be easily applied to make someone feel calmer, stronger or more vitalized in a general way.

Many of the hands on healing techniques are based on ideologies or belief in the support of "higher" powers such as saints, angels, helpful spirits of any kind, or an avatar or God, in the case of believers in Jesus Christ. Of course, all these techniques can cause a spontaneous remission if the healer's intention is strong enough. But how often will we be able to experience such a miracle? It is actually very rare to see one. Even so, hands on healing can be a very powerful therapeutic tool to relieve spine problems if we learn how to apply it correctly to a specific problem. In order to be a successful hands-on healer one has to meet three essential preconditions. First we need to reactivate our inherent ability to perceive life energy either through our sense of touch or to literally see it with our eyes. Both these are not miracles and can be easily with a bit of discipline by those who are willing to undergo a specific training for this. The next chapter has detailed instructions about how to achieve this.

Secondly we have to learn to understand how a specific health problem – in our case a spine problem – has come into being. That means to possess knowledge about the anatomy and physiology of the area we want to treat. We also need to know what causes pain in the people we are treating – is it just muscular tension, or is it some kind of degenerative change? We really do have to do some serious research about this if we want to work systematically in this field. Most of the information we need we can be found if we have access to a doctor's diagnosis. It is best to base it at least on an X-ray or even better on a MRI scan. The only thing we will not find there are emotional or mental reasons which may have caused the physical problem in the first place. These can be detected through observation and by speaking to the client. We can also gain a lot of background information by analyzing the client's energy field.

Thirdly, we have to acquire specific techniques to directly manipulate the energy fields of our clients. This is necessary, for example, to reduce inflammation, to create more space around a spinal nerve, or to pad out a degenerated intervertebral disc. All these applications are much easier to learn when we take into consideration that it is basically simply a case of releasing energy where it is blocked or over-full, and boosting the energy where there is too little. There will be detailed instructions for this later. You will learn techniques to accumulate life energy, draw it out from somewhere and transfer it elsewhere, penetrate tissues and change specific frequencies. For the moment let us have a closer look at how hands-on healing works on a client. What are the hard facts beyond beliefs and miracles?

Effects of Hands on Healing As Explained By Modern Science

Although there is a body of medical research studying the effects of healing on patients suffering from a number of different illnesses, in practice orthodox medicine generally denies the existence of healing energy. In many instances, when there have been cases where healing has occurred without a comprehensible medical reason, it is said to be a *"placebo effect"*. The placebo effect means that a strong belief in something can cause dramatic changes within a person. Any cure will work if the patient believes strongly enough in its healing potential.

At the end of the Second World War when Germany was on the verge of collapse, doctors in mobile army surgical hospitals often ran out of morphine. Desperate to ease the pain of seriously injured soldiers they gave them infusions of physiological saline telling them that it was morphine. Surprisingly this worked. Most of the severely wounded soldiers experienced a dramatic relief of pain only because they believed that morphine had been used on them. This can be interpreted that a transfer of information about the effects of morphine had taken place in brains of the wounded soldier's without them having taken it as a material substance.

A lot of research has been done into the placebo effect since then and many studies published on this topic have shown amazing results. It has proven to be of great advantage to patients who suffered severe side effects from regular medications. For example, in a number of studies conducted on pregnant women who could not tolerate a lot of medication, they were given some placebo pills consisting mainly of pure dextrose which were found to give relief to nearly 80% of the participants.

The placebo effect may appear to some of us as a kind of "magic". Another but more negative aspect of the same effect can be found to be just as true. The moment an individual strongly believes in the existence of black magic or voodoo it is possible to affect him through this. As soon as a person is strongly convinced or believes in the effects of a medication or a treatment or even in "psychic attack" then it is bound to bring about dramatic changes within his or her brain metabolism. As a result of this the signals and commands given by the hormonal glands will cause an adjustment to several body functions which in some cases may lead to a miraculous spontaneous remission. These changes can occur merely from a simple conversation between a patient and a doctor or therapist of any kind. From this we can easily understand how important it is for a patient to feel that their doctor or therapist really cares about their well being.

The doctor can influence their patient with their intention to help, whether it is genuine or not. The patient's trust and belief in the doctor's ability to help opens the door and influences their condition. All these are a result of the changes within the brain where neuropeptides act under the same laws as lightquants.

Hands-on healing also causes such changes but its effects can not be explained by this idea of the placebo effect alone, it involves much more. To come to a closer understanding of the whole concept of hands-on healing we have to overcome the Aristotelian logic which many of us still accept as being the ultimate truth and the objective reality. Unfortunately there is no such a thing as an objective reality nor can the common logic of "either / or" be true.

The outlook on reality has drastically being changed by the work of *Bohr; Einstein, Plank, Schrödinger* and many others.

Unfortunately this change of paradigms within physics has neither reached academic medicine nor to the majority of humans' thoughts. The main reason for this may be that the concepts of quantum mechanics seem to be totally confusing and irrational if one is used to thinking the Aristotelian way, as most of us have been taught to do. We can simply say that matter and energy is simultaneously the same thing at the same time. Realizing this fact is very important for hands-on healing because when a healer is changing the energy field, changes take place in matter as well.

The best way to prove this idea is to look at the ground-breaking experiment called *Schrödinger's Cat*. *Schrödinger*, a Viennese physicist and Nobel Prize winner, proposed a hypothetical experiment whereby a cat was locked in a cage. In this hypothetical experiment, the cat was given a pill without the researcher knowing whether this pill was poisonous or harmless. If the pill had been toxic the cat would have died within half an hour. As it was not possible to look into the cage because it was completely covered, and the cat inside had an exactly a 50:50 chance of survival, nobody could say if the cat was dead or alive until the cage had been opened again. This highly theoretical experiment concluded that as long as nobody looked in to the cage, then the cat was both dead and alive at the same time. The moment that somebody opened the cage and looked in, they would be able to identify the state of the cat: either dead or alive. According to the quantum theory, which is also applied to describing the motion of energy as simultaneously waves and particles, this would then mean that for the person who was in a room next door, the cat was still both dead and alive at the same time so long as the person in the laboratory had not told them what had happened to the cat. As long as the actual state of the cat had not been determined by an observer the cat continues to be dead or alive simultaneously.

So how does all this theory relate to back pain?

Any living biological unit, such as the human body, is made up of electromagnetic waves and material particles at the same time. Therefore, every change in the material structure of the particles will cause the same change in the electromagnetic structure at the same time, and vice versa. For example, if a scar remains a problem after a surgery, we should take into consideration that it will have an electromagnetic structure as well. Because it is not possible to define what is exactly causing the pain on a physical level, there is a possibility of relieving the pain if the scar is treated as an electromagnetic structure through the directed care hands-on healing method.

A third component also has to be taken into consideration: This is the field of biophotons emitted by a body. This vital energy field is the sum of biophotons emitted by each single cell of a body and works as a medium between two or more organisms. This *aura* is responsible for the transfer of information between two biological systems. If a healer is able to perceive the aura emitted by another person, they will have access to all the information about the actual state of this individual. The healer also has the opportunity to change that information, which in turn may cause a change in the electromagnetic and material structure of a person's body.

In the case of the problematic scar mentioned previously, this would mean that we have a painful scar which exists simultaneously as a material structure of particles as well as an electromagnetic structure of waves. The reason for the pain cannot be defined precisely by analyzing the material structure but rather through analyzing the biophotons emitted by this scar. Using the senses of a healer, one can locate the problem, for example, as a tickling feeling of heat on the healer's palm while scanning the scar. The healer will now be able to initiate a change within the aura, by "rewriting" the information and transfering it back into the scar tissue. The result would be a change in the electromagnetic wave structure of the scar which in turn changes the material structure of the particles, leading to pain relief.

This is where the placebo effect has become a reality as a successful intentional transfer of information on an electromagnetic level. As a human being has a physical, mental, and emotional, body and a "soul", this intentional information transfer can be done on each of these levels separately or on all of them together.

Tools Needed to Practice Hands On Healing
The ability to heal others by laying hands on them is a natural gift inherent in all of us. This is a lot like playing the violin. Theoretically everybody can do it, but to play it really well one needs to have a lot of discipline, even if one is extraordinarily gifted in this field. It is generally not easy to be a successful hands-on healer, but to successfully treat a specialized area such as back problems demands even more. You have to first fix your own physical hardware, which is your body, re-educate your perception to its original state, and later learn how to manipulate life energy on very small areas within the spine. For example, you should be able to work on a spinal nerve which has been squashed as a result of a prolapsed disc.

To practice hands-on healing professionally you need to be in good physical condition because it can become very exhausting at times. You will need endurance and muscle strength to channel strong healing energies through your limbs in the way that water flows through a rubber hose. You will also need to change the frequency of the life energy stream by contracting specific muscle groups. Your spine and your joints will have to be flexible to optimize the energy flow. Do not, however, worry unduly as increasing your endurance doesn't mean that you have to become a triathlon athlete, or developing muscle strength does not mean becoming a body builder. All it means is that an increased flexibility of your spine and main joints will lead to better results when you do hands-on healing.

It makes no difference whether you begin as a healer as a 20-year-old active young man or a 65-year-old retired person now winding down having spent a whole lifetime working hard. All that matters is that as you work on improving your abilities to enhance your healing skills wherever there are deficits. An older person who may have less physical agility probably has some advantage over the younger ones as they would have acquired more experience in their lives and be able to successfully handle different people on a psychological level.

There are many ways you can build up your physical endurance and muscle strength. By walking forty minutes each day you will be able to achieve amazing results. As you continue to improve, try to increase the distance covered within this forty minute stretch each day. It will not only build up your physical endurance but also strengthen your lungs and heart and help to reduce your weight. If you prefer cycling then you can achieve similar results by exercising for two hours a day. To optimize the effects of your training you should rest every third day. Although cycling requires more time it has the advantage of building strong leg muscles as you work on increasing your endurance level.

All the muscles which bend or straighten your hip are connected to the first chakra and are very important in healing work. This is because in the directed care system of hands-on healing we work mainly with the earth's magnetic field to achieve changes on a physical level. Our physical body is made up of elements from Mother Earth and if this cannot bring about healing in some form, nothing else can.

When the soles of our feet are on the floor we are physically connected to the earth's energy field. The stronger our leg muscles are the more energy we can draw in and can then transfer to somebody else who needs it. Well-trained stomach muscles are necessary if you are doing professional healing work as it provides emotional stability and immunity against taking on other people's emotions. It also helps the healer to remain grounded and not be carried away by a client's inner fears and needs. If a healer identifies too closely with other people's emotions and makes them their own, in the long run it will drain their life energy and affect their physical condition as well. If a healer loses their grounding or becomes ungrounded, they will begin to lose their electromagnetic shape as an individual as they unconsciously take on someone else's electromagnetic shape as well as the patterns of physical diseases of their clients. This explains why the second chakra, which is the stomach area, works as an emotional centre as well as an electromagnetic equivalent of our physical immune system.

Eating the right kind of food optimizes the results of training to be a healer. Healing work speeds up the cellular metabolism and requires an adequate support of vitamins, mineral traces and also a higher intake of proteins than is usually needed. Proteins are not only important in building muscles but also in building up all the neurotransmitters. They will be needed for the different brain functions directly involved in hands-on healing as well as in increasing your brain's ability to perceive life energy fields. The problem is that it is hard to get the required amount and quality of proteins from plants alone. Many people have strong moral opinions about eating meat based on ideologies or their personal beliefs. It is true that meat from animals raised under certain industrial conditions will not provide the necessary quality. We also have the same problem with vegetables, fruits and grains. Organically or biologically grown food should be chosen, whether they are animals or plants. We should never forget that food not only provides us with nutrients but also contains an electromagnetic wave structure which gives information to our body of light.

The hip area in the temple of man represents his physical body and the stomach area represents his emotional body. A healer who has worked on building strong leg muscles will be well grounded to the earth. His strong stomach muscles will also provide him with emotional stability and a better immune system and in addition it will prevent him from having lower back problems. All the exercises mentioned in the earlier chapters are also suitable for professional healers to build their endurance and muscle strength.

Just as the pelvis region connects the healer to the earth, the upper part which is the shoulder and the arms will be used to interact with a client's energy field. Our hands are not only our main instrument of transmitting live energy to someone else but also a very important sensual organ. Having a flexible neck is important as it provides the whole range of movement for our "antennas" that is: our eyes, ears and the nose. You have all the exercises needed for the neck and shoulder region in the second part of this book.

Being physically fit is a prerequisite to move life energy. We should learn first to move it consciously within our own bodies before doing so on others. We can use the following exercises: the Tree Stand, the Snake Movement and the meditation to help balance our life energy along the spine as mentioned in chapter five.

After becoming familiar with these exercises we can begin to work on the next essential requirement to become a powerful healer. While exercising, do not put yourself under too much pressure to reach your goal, rather exercise for the sheer pleasure of it and increase your awareness of the beauty and joy of being alive. Exercising with discipline and joy will make you a successful healer. You will develop a kinaesthetic and visual perception of life energy that means to really physically perceive and not merely imagine or visualize life energy.

CHAPTER 8

How to Perceive Life Energy

Developing Altered Sensory Perceptions

What do you expect when you think of seeing an aura? Do you have a specific idea of what an aura should look like, and if so, where does this idea come from? Did you form your expectations from something you have read about in a book? There are many books on the market with explanations about how an aura ought to look. Most of these ideas are based on the work done by Annie Besant and Charles Leadbeater. In the 1920s sources from India and Tibet were interpreted and published in a book called "*The Chakras*". This book has been a source of inspiration for many writers in this field. Nowadays quantum physics and modern psychology give us new insights on this topic.

Let us take a look of how a group of people in a room respond when they look at a chair. Without any doubt everyone will see a chair but not everyone will see the same chair. The image of the chair is assembled from electromagnetic and biochemical stimuli within your brain. We do not all have an identical pair of eyes, eyesight or brain functions. Every human being is unique and so are his perceptions. This means that everyone present in the room will create his own distinctive image of the chair.

Our perception is always a result of learning. As an infant we explore the world first with our sense of smell to recognize our mother's milk, our lips when we drink the milk, and later with our little fingers when we feel her skin. In this early stage babies define their self image by sound when they cry. It is only much later that babies fully develop their eyesight. Just as a baby begins to experience the world we have to follow a similar path if we want to rediscover our abilities to perceive life energy.

When you experience any kind of sensory perception, groups

of nerve endings are stimulated. Specific nerve endings within our skin react with an infinitesimal electrical discharge when we touch somebody or something. This also happens when rays of light hit our retina. Such electrical impulses form patterns which are forwarded to the brain where it triggers a chemical reaction and leads to a complex interaction of nerve cells giving us instantly an image of what we have "seen" or "touched". The more often a particular cluster of brain cells is stimulated the more it will be reinforced, which leads us to the conclusion that sensory perception can be improved through training.

When you accompany an experienced hunter into the jungle you will be surprised at how much information he is able to gather from the environment which you have absolutely no access to. He is able to see things that you did not even know existed. This increased awareness is because of his specialized training and experience over a long period of time. As the hunter's inexperienced companion, even if you are unable to see any deer at all you have to agree with the hunter that the deer exists.

This is the difference and the problem when we speak about seeing so called invisible things like a human energy field.

When we speak about human perception it does not only consist of individual perception but also to a great degree, a common perception which is based on the cultural environment that one lives in. To give you an example: When Columbus and his ships appeared on the horizon for the first time the native people were not able to see them because in the specific cultural reality of the Native Americans, sailing ships did not exist within their spectrum of experience so they literally did not see them. Some time elapsed before the first Indian was able to see with his eyes what he had first felt only as a gut feeling of something unlike anything he had experienced before appearing on the horizon. The moment one of the Indians was able to expand his perception, others in the whole tribe could suddenly see the sailing ships too.

There is no consensus within our society about the existence of a human energy field. In the scientific community only a small number of physicists and other people involved in the "spiritual" community accept the idea that such a phenomenon exists. Unfortunately the majority of our society for a variety reasons such as ideological, religious and pre-quantum scientific theories, still deny the possibility of the existence of a human energy field. As a result of this most of our children grow up without getting a chance to develop their inherent perception of life energy. There are of course other cultures such as the South American Indians and native people from Asia, Africa and Australia who have developed a different outlook on this topic. In all these cultures the concept of life energy is not only integrated but it forms the basis of most medical treatments there. In Traditional Chinese Medicine, the Tibetan medicine or the Indian Aryuvedic medicine treatments which bring about a change in the physical matter are given by influencing the electromagnetic waves of the body of light. The most important precondition in making a diagnosis about diseases as well as measuring any progress achieved by the treatment is to have a tool to sense this body of light.

In the oriental medicine such as acupuncture, specific qualities of life energy are assessed by pulse diagnosis. By sensing the pulses on specific spots above the wrist the practitioner assesses the state of balance in the individual field of a patient's life energy. Each spot represents a specific quality and the different qualities felt on the spots above the wrist provide information about the client's health condition. When the practitioner applies this information to the system of the Five Elements he or she has a clear idea of where to find the disturbances within the energy body and how to sort it out by using acupuncture or herbal medicine.

Even if these methods are often very successful in curing an illness it has the disadvantage of being based more on an abstract notion of life energy which needs to be studied for a long time if you want to be a successful acupuncturist. Without using any kind of sophisticated system anyone can affect a remarkable change on an effected area. The essential precondition is to be able to perceive life energy directly through our sensory organs. When you are able to directly perceive life energy you can clearly define the area where you have to work on and will be able to check immediately if your treatment has been successful or not.

In order to be able to perceive or 'see' life energy you have to do what you have done when you were a baby. We have to continuously build up and reinforce the neuronal networks within our cerebral cortex which are responsible in giving us pictures or impressions of touching life energy.

Kinaesthetic Perception

When we want to regain our ability to perceive life energy through our senses we have to develop our sensory organs and re-train our brain by learning continuously by experience. Take some small pebbles and lay them on a plain surface in different forms, either as a circle, a triangle, a triangle within a circle, a square; or try whatever shape comes to your mind. Now place the palm of one of your hands at a distance of about 10-15 cm over the geometric shape you have chosen. Observe closely to see if you feel any sensations on your palm. Usually there will be some kind of a warm sensation or a kind of tickling. Try to scan some other shapes and see if you are able to recognize any differences on your palm.

What has been described above is one of the ways that Native American Indians train their children to perceive life energy as a sensory sensation. Many adults who try to feel objects without actually touching them may in the beginning fail to feel anything. This is because the nerve endings in the skin of their hands have not been stimulated by electromagnetic sensations for a long time. We literally have to "wake them up" if we want them to react not only to a physical stimulus but also to a much more fragile stimulus of electromagnetic waves such as fields of biophotons.

Exercise 1: Reawakening the Nerve Endings in your Hand

Sit upright on the edge of a chair and raise your right arm. Bend your elbow so that the back of your hand comes close to your right shoulder and that your forearm is relaxed. Spread your fingers slightly apart.

Then begin to bend and straighten the first phalanx of your middle finger. Make only very tiny movements. Keep all other fingers still moving only the first phalanx of your middle finger and later move it together with the first phalanx of your ring finger.

Slowly expand this type of movement to all the five fingers of your hand but continue to be aware of bending and straightening only the first phalanx of your fingers. After a while you will experience a warm sensation on your palm. This is a good sign because it confirms that you are doing the exercise correctly.

As you continue to move the first phalanxes of your fingers expand this feeling of warmth into your wrist and into your forearm. From there you move this sensation of warmth to your elbow, your upper arm, your shoulder and finally to your head. You should do this exercise with both your hand for as long as you are able to create a warm sensation within your palm and are able to expand it to your head.

Exercise 2: Experiencing the "Two Layers"

Stand on the floor with your weight equally distributed on both feet. Bend your knees a little and raise your arms to the middle of your chest. Bend your elbows a little and turn your wrists so that your palms are facing each other.

Now move your hand apart as far as you can. As you very slowly move your palms back towards each other, be aware of any sensation which might occur on your palm. At some point there will be a kind of elastic resistance which can be felt between your hands as you move them closer towards each other you will come to a point where you will experience the same sensation again. Repeat this over and over again until you can feel a clear sensation with both distances.

Maintain the same position but relax your arms along your body. Now bring your whole weight to the balls of your feet and then put your weight back on the whole soles. Repeat this six times. Now breathe in sharply and contract your anus at the same time. Breathe out and relax. Repeat this twelve times.

Move your palms towards each other and check to see if you can feel the same sensation of resistance even more intensely than before. Repeat this several times with both distances.

At this stage your nerve endings are ready to receive electro magnetic stimuli from another organism and forward them into your brain. For the next series of exercises you will need to work with a partner.

Exercise 3: Scanning the Head

Ask your partner to sit on a chair and stand behind him. Raise your hands to your partner's temples and hold them at a distance of approximately 18 inches or half a metre apart. Now slowly bring your hands closer towards the temples and be aware of any kind of sensation you feel there. Do you feel a kind of elastic resistance? Is the distance of this resistance equal on the right and the left side of your partner's head? Repeat this exercise and check as long as you have a clear sensation on your palms.

Exercise 4: Scanning the whole Body

Ask your partner to lie on his back; support his head with a flat cushion and place a rolled up blanket under his knees. Stand on your partner's right side. Clap your hands and rub your palms vigorously against each other.

Now scan with one or with both your palms the whole body starting from the feet to the head. Begin from a distance of approximately 15 inches or 40 centimetres from the surface of the body, drawing closer and closer until you reach the inner layer which would be a distance of approximately four inches or 10 centimetres from the surface of the body. Observe closely all the changes you can feel as you scan the different areas at varying distances. Do this with as many people as possible to compare how their energy feels and also to compare the different areas of the body scanned from various distances.

Exercise 5: Scanning the Spine

Sit behind your partner and hold your palm (left or right whichever you prefer) at a distance of approximately four inches or 10 centimetres over your partner's sacrum. Check if you can feel any sensation there. You may find a kind of resistance, a tickling sensation or a feeling of warmth on your palm, or maybe even a combination of all of these. Place your hands over the sacrum until you can clearly feel a sensation.

Now keeping the same distance of about ten centimetres, move your hands up towards the head feeling the sensations on each single vertebra. Check if you can pick up any other kind of sensation especially in the intersections between the vertebrae where the discs are situated. See if there are spots where you feel more heat, or does it have a sticky kind of quality instead of an elastic resistance. Check to see if there is any kind of aggressive needle like quality present somewhere in the spine area. Are there any areas where you can feel a cold sensation or areas which do not seem to have any sensation at all as if there was a "hole" in the life energy field?

Shake your hands vigorously to discharge energy after scanning another person's energy field.

Try all these exercises with as many different people as possible. If you find noticeable sensations of any kind discuss them with your partner to find out if he is aware of any problems there.

After having practiced these exercises successfully you will now be able to perceive fields of life energy with your hands. When you are able to do this kinaesthetically you will be able to see life energy with your eyes as well.

Visual Perception

When we usually refer to seeing, we usually mean physically seeing the visible light spectrum found within electromagnetic waves which are on a wavelength between 380 nanometers (violet) and 780 nanometers (red). Our brain interprets the stimuli on the retina within this spectrum and produces the pictures we see. This is what we call eyesight. Among the majority of human beings there exists a common agreement about what is visible and what is not and for the majority it is only the spectrum of visible light. Quantum physics describes light as a stream of photons, whether it is in the visible spectrum or not. When the source of light is a stream of biophotons, it will continue to be invisible to us as long as we try to apply the same technique to see this type of light as we do with visible light. The reason why it does not work is because a stream of biophotons has a different wavelength than the visible light spectrum. This means it stimulates the retina in a different way and our brain is not used to interpreting this kind of stimuli as a picture.

We have learned that it is possible to feel a field of biophotons through nerve endings within our fingers and to interpret and differentiate these sensations within our brain. In almost the same manner we can re-train our retina and brain to get a visual impression of life energy. A visual perception means not just imagining or visualizing life energy but really having a sensation similar to the experience you have when you touch fields consisting of biophotons. The reason why it is much more difficult to see than to scan a biomagnetic field with your hands is that you are unable to separate "visible" light from the streams of photons of another wavelength. When you touch you know exactly whether you are touching the physical body or the body of light. Whereas when you look at someone's energy field you have to find out how to separate different wavelengths while looking at them simultaneously so that your brain is able to produce two images at the same time – one for the physical body and one for the body of light.

Exercise 1: Switching the View

Sit on a chair and relax. Raise your arm and look at the palm of your hand. Observe closely the shape of your palm and your fingers. Look at all the different nuances of color you can find within the skin of your fingers and palm. For example look at the white areas on your skin, the red or maybe the blue tones and then focus on all of them simultaneously. Look at the different lines engraved on the surface of your skin observing as many details as possible. Look at all the details at the same time then view them separately from each other. Now relax your arm and rest for a little while.

Once again lift your arm so that you can look at your palm. Keep it at a maximum distance from your eyes as possible. Focusing now on your eyes and from your eyes send a ray of light to your palm until you have a clear sensation of warmth there.

Then retract this ray of light as far as possible back into your system by circling life energy on your navel point (as mentioned in Chapter Five on the *Exercise to Balance Life Energy along the Spine*) until the sensation of warmth within your palm disappears. Repeat this for several times then relax and rest for a while.

Lift your arm once again and keep your palm at the maximum possible distance from your eyes. Once more look at your palm and send a ray of light but now do not focus on the palm but instead see if you can sense a kind of resistance on your eyeballs as you reach a certain distance from the palm. This resistance should feel very similar to what you feel within your hands when you use them to scan someone's field of life energy.

Try this until you have a clear sensation on your eyeballs as they touch the surface of your hands life energy field. Be conscious as to how far away you are from the physical surface of your palm before you can feel a resistance on your eyes. Now you can check your visual impression kinaesthetically by moving your palms towards each other. Do you feel a resistance at the same distance from the surface of your palm as you felt with your eyes? Now from your eyes send a ray of light to the back of your hand until you can feel clearly your eyes "touching" the surface area of the field of biophotons there. Relax and rest for a while.

Raise your arm and look at your palm. Focus first on its physical appearance then change the focus and touch with the eyes the electromagnetic field of your palm. Switch between these two tasks as often as possible until you are able to do it easily. Then do both simultaneously: Look at the palm and at the same time touch it's Aura with your eyes. Relax and rest for a while.

Once you have experienced consciously this sensation of touching the aura with your eyes you have initiated a chain reaction within your brain. The truth is that you practice this kind of perception unconsciously all the time but now you are more aware of a different form of stimulation on your retina. This is nothing new at all for your brain. As a child this was as common as your "normal" eyesight to you. For different reasons most people lose these skills when as little children they begin to stand up and walk around. As you begin to remember what was once self evident then you will reinforce all the neuronal clusters within your brain which are responsible for creating images of life energy.

The following exercise is designed to support this reinforcement by differentiating your perceptions at one hand and on the other helping you to develop an altered awareness of your spine. For this exercise you need a partner.

Exercise 2: Enlarging your Perception of Life Energy along the Spine

Observe your partner as s/he walks around the room. Look closely at each detail for example the way your partner moves their pelvis and spine. Are their movements flexible or stiff? Can you identify any specific restricted segments as you watch their movements? Is there anything distinctive within your partner's movements which may be a manifestation of an underlying emotional or mental problem?

Now sit behind your partner and from your eyes send a ray of light to their sacrum until you can feel a resistance of the life energy field touching your eyes. Remain there for a while and check if you can "see" any movement either a flow or a circular movement. Observe whether this movement is round or more elliptical. Are you able to see any color there? Do this without any pressure or force on yourself. Do not expect anything, just relax and observe. It takes time until your perception develops.

As you move from one vertebra to the next, observe any distinctive features you see there. Do you feel a continuous flow of life energy with an equal quality of resistance everywhere or are there some places where you experience a difference? Maybe you can see a kind of bend or a bulge somewhere, especially in the area between the vertebrae, where the discs are situated. If you sense more extensive blockages within the field it may be an expression of an increased muscular tension there. Observe the tension in the muscles and at the same time any disturbances of the life energy field there. As far as possible deepen your perception of matter and energy at the same time.

As you come closer and closer to the head compare the basic density of the life energy field and see if it is different from the lower areas of the spine. As you scan with your eyes and move up the spine be aware that you may see different colors spontaneously. At this point focus only on observing but not analyzing anything. Become more and more aware of details of every single vertebra from the bottom to the top.

Learn to distinguish how different tissues such as bones, ligaments, cartilage or muscles emit different qualities of Life energy and sense this closely by differentiating if possible with your eyes. All these need a lot of experience, experience which you will only get with constant training over a period of time. Use as many persons as you can for your observations. If anything unusual occurs discuss it with your partner to find out whether they are suffering from any problems which correspond to the observations you have made.

CHAPTER 9

How to Transfer Life Energy

Grounding

To "be grounded" is a phrase used in the hands-on healing technique which basically means having a down to earth approach towards what you are achieving as a healer. This has a number of different meanings for a hands-on healer. To be grounded is when a healer has his feet firmly on the ground and is actually able to perceive and transfer life energy and is not merely doing this in his imagination. For this reason real "grounding" requires the healer to continuously check if the transfer of life energy is actually taking place or is it merely a figment of his imagination. The healer in a sense needs to control the flow of life energy within their own body as well as that of their client. The areas which are being treated have to be analyzed accurately again and again to see if any changes have occurred in the client's energy field. For a healing session to be successful it is necessary to work constantly on developing the skills needed to perceive life energy.

There is another very important reason why a healer must be firmly grounded. The healer has to be aware that in order to bring about any physical changes in their client's energy field, he or she has to be conscious of the fact that all material things that exist on earth is born out of Mother Earth. Through her biomagnetic patterns the earth shapes the sunlight – the source of all material within our sun system – into matter. To repair a field of life energy that has been damaged, a healer has to rebuild it to its original shape. This means s/he has to provide the information drawn from the earth and transfer it into the client's energy field to repair as far as possible any damage in the physical structure, for example in treating a degenerated disc. Looking at it from this angle it is clear that a healer has to be closely and consciously in contact with the earth's biomagnetic field to really bring about changes on a physical level within the client's body.

What are some of the practical things that a healer can do so as to be really grounded? The first thing to do is to stop living in your mental body, in your thoughts, imagination and fantasies but to start realizing the reality of your physical body. The simplest way is to move as much as possible and spend time in nature, for example going for a walk in the woods or by the seashore. Become conscious of your movements and your physical body. Become aware of your close connection to nature and that you are an inseparable part of the earth. The more conscious you are of your relation to the earth the more you will gain access to the mysteries of life which go far beyond dogmas and beliefs and will take you back to the physical and spiritual reality. This is what it really means to be grounded.

The parts of your body which are most closely connected to the surface of the earth are the soles of your feet. When you do healing work your soles are always on the floor whether you are standing or sitting. The soles of your feet are a "gateway" for the additional earth energy that you later transmit to your clients. At the same time, your soles also work as a pathway for any kind of energy you draw out from our client which is send back through your feet to the earth. This way you avoid being affected by the bioenergetic information of any kind of disease which you remove from our clients. Instead of taking it in your own system you bring it down to the earth where it is neutralised and becomes pure energy again. To work effectively and successfully as a hands-on-healer it is important to ensure that the centres in your soles are opened up to its maximum, especially when you are a beginner in healing work. You will benefit greatly when you prepare yourself by doing the following exercise before you begin a healing session.

Exercises to Help you Prepare for a Healing Session:

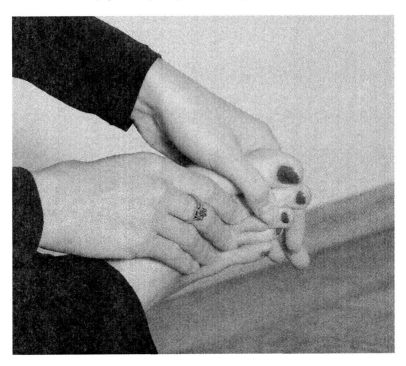

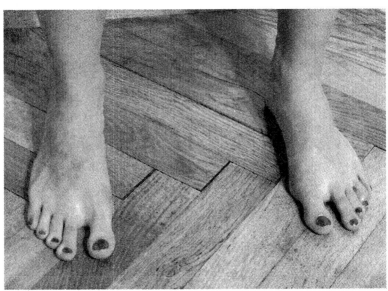

Sit on a chair and place your lower right leg on the thigh of your left leg. Grab your toes and rub them one by one. Then make a fist with your left hand and roll it several times over your right sole from the heel to the toes. Next hold the ball of your foot in both hands press your thumbs against the sole while pulling the sides of your foot towards each other so that the instep becomes arched.

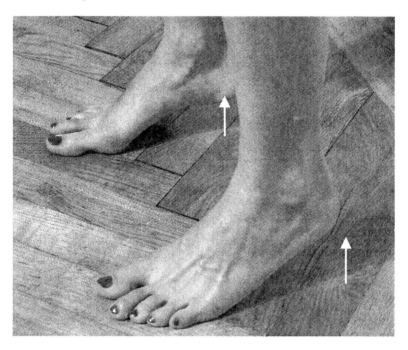

Stand up and focus on how your soles touch the floor. Is your weight equally distributed on the whole sole or are you standing more on your heels or the balls of your feet? Check and see if you tend to put your weight more on the inner or the outer edge of your feet. Correct your position until you can sense both you soles touching the floor completely and experience them as being suction cups.

Now breathe in and at the same time lift your heels up and put all your weight on your forefeet. Breathe out and bring your heels down to the floor again. Repeat this a number of times.

How to Collect Life Energy

Once you are familiar with the basic grounding techniques you are ready for the next stage of your journey to become a healer. If you are well-grounded and connected to the earth you can easily draw as much life energy as much as you need from the earth's electromagnetic field which reaches a distance of approximately 60,000 kilometres into space towards the sun and 600,000 kilometres away from the sun. This will give you an idea of the magnitude of the energy field that you are dealing with.

First you have to learn to charge your own energy field fully and transmit only the surplus energy, otherwise you would exhaust yourself very quickly because people suffering from different health problems, particularly those who are in tremendous pain, lose a large amount of life energy through the pain, and when you treat them you are the one who has to recharge their energy field. This can only be done without harming yourself in the long term when you are grounded which means being linked to the greatest available source of life energy.

To understand how this exchange of energy works let us look at an example of a concentration of a salt solution – one is highly concentrated and the other is more diluted so less concentrated. As soon as these two are mixed the concentration of the salt in both becomes equalized. From this example one can observe how it is possible to balance out life energy when it is in a state of being full or empty. What this means in terms of healing work is that the systems of both the healer and his client should be saturated as much as possible with life energy at the end of a hands-on healing session. The following exercise will help you to completely and consciously recharge your own system. Practicing this exercise before beginning healing work on a client will benefit healers who are beginners with little experience in this kind of work. Later when you have developed a routine you will be able to create the same effect by just initiating it mentally.

To achieve the best results you should practice this after having done the exercises to Balance Life Energy Along your Spine in Chapter Five as well as the Tree Stand exercise in Chapter Six. Once you are familiar with these you will be able to clearly perceive the flow of life energy within your body which is the most important requirement for benefiting fully from the following exercise.

Exercise: Collecting Life energy within your Own System
Stand on the floor with your feet shoulder width apart parallel to each other. Be aware that your weight is equally distributed on both your feet. Bend your knees so far that they are in line with the tips of your toes. Spread your knees apart as if you are sitting on a horse. Then move your sacrum a little inward so that you stretch your lumbar spine. Bring your chin closer to your throat so that the rest of your spine is stretched.

Focus on the balls of your feet and feel them to be suction cups and as you breathe in let Life energy flow consciously from the ground into your body. Breathe out. Repeat this until you clearly feel the sensation of an upward flowing movement inside your legs.

Breathe in once more and as your lift your arms in front of your body to shoulder height pull the life energy up from the ground through your legs into your stomach and to your chest. Breathe out and push the life energy out from there through your arms as your bend up your palms outwards and straighten your arms forward.

Slowly bring your arms back to the starting position. Repeat these movements until you can feel a clear sensation of a flow through your body as you breathe in. As you breathe out you should feel it flowing from your arms to your palms creating a warm sensation there.

Pushing and Pulling

Any kind of hands-on healing, no matter how sophisticated it may be, is based on one simple principle: to complement life energy where is too little of it and to draw out or release life energy from areas where it accumulates and becomes too much. A lack of life energy in a specific area would mean that the vital functions in the related tissues are dramatically restricted. An accumulation causes an overabundance of life energy which may manifest itself, for example, as an inflammatory process. In order to rebalance the body of light you need to use the basic techniques of pushing and pulling.

What does this technique of pushing and pulling imply? Pushing is the conscious and directed transmission of life energy from the earth through a healer into a client. Pulling is the conscious and directed reverse flow of life energy from the client through the healer back to the earth.

These pushing and pulling techniques can be done with the healer's whole body, the hands, and fingers or through the healer's eyes. In order to treat spine problems we will focus primarily on our abilities to move life energy in both directions through our hands and fingers. For the following exercises you need a partner.

Exercise 1: Pushing Life Energy into a Partner

Sit on chairs face to face with your partner. Lay your palms on the palms of your partner.

As you breathe in pull life energy from the ground through

your soles into your body. As you breathe out with your intention push life energy out through your arms and palms into the palms and arms of your partner. Follow attentively the flow of life energy and extend your awareness as deeply as possible into your partner's body.

Repeat this until your partner can clearly sense the stream of life energy moving into his body. This may be an increased feeling of warmth or as a kind of flowing movement.

Exercise 2: Pulling Life Energy from a Partner
Some of you may find the pulling movement much more difficult than the pushing. It is always surprising to see how easily people manage to give life energy and how hard it is for them to take it. This has a lot to do with religious beliefs, cultural conditioning which rule our subconsciousness much more than expected. For example women are educated to serve and to give. The concept of taking makes them feel guilty. It is a taboo, as some of us will have a hard time learning to pull energy away from somewhere.

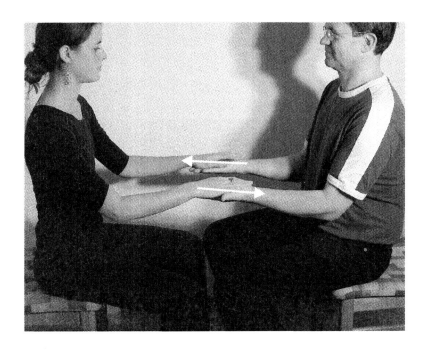

Sit on a chair face to face to your partner. Place your palms under the palms of your partner.

As you breathe in, pull life energy out from the palms of your partner and as you breathe out send it through your soles into the ground. You can now lay your palms on that of your partner and see if you find it easier for you to pull life energy in this position.

Repeat this until you can clearly feel the flow of life energy from your partner's palms into your own arms.

Exercise 3: Creating a Cyclic Flow by Pushing and Pulling at the Same Time

Sit on chairs face to face with your partner. Place your right palm on your partners left palm and your partner should lay his right palm on your left.

As you breathe in take life energy from the ground through your soles into your body. As you breathe out intentional push life energy out through your right arm and palm into your partner's left palm and arm. Then breathe in and pull life energy from your partner's right arm and palm into your left palm.

Repeat this until the both of you clearly feel the stream of life moving through your arms and shoulders in a cycle.

Now reverse the direction. As you pull with the left hand push at the same time the life energy with your right hand into your partner.

Continue to repeat by reversing the direction of life energy flow until the both of you can clearly feel a change of direction when life energy moves within your arms and shoulders.

Flushing
Whenever a healer wants to strengthen a specific organ or tissue they should use the Flushing technique to achieve the best results. This technique deletes "destructive" information within the body of light and provides electromagnetic information which activates an increased function and proper reduplication of cells within the tissue that has been treated.

If you want to cover a large organ, for example the liver, or a big joint such as the hip or a shoulder, you can flush with the whole palms of both your hands.

When you want to treat the spine you have to also face the challenge of working on much smaller areas such as inter vertebral discs or the delicate intervertebral joints. We have to therefore use our fingertips when we want on these small and delicate areas. The following exercises will enable you to use both: your palms and fingertips. To practice this you need to work with a partner.

Exercise 1: Flushing the Right Shoulder

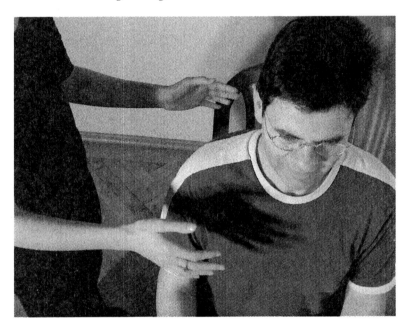

Stand on the right side of your partner and place your left hand in front and your right hand on the back of your partner's right shoulder at a distance of approximately 12 inches or 30 centimetres.

As you move your palms towards your partner's right shoulder scan the whole joint accurately. In addition use your eyes to get a visual perception of the life energy field of the shoulder. Record whatever you can feel and see in this area, for example, the density of this field, its flexibility, and whether you find an increased sensation of warmth, heat or cold, or if there is a tickling sensation on yours palms and any other things that may draw your attention there.

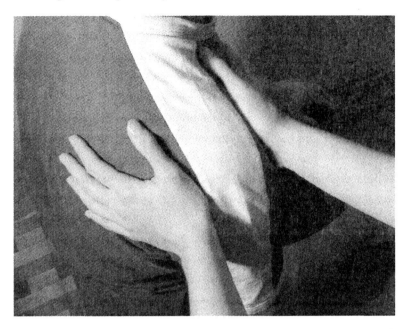

Now place your right hand on the back of your partner's right shoulder joint and your left hand on the front. Breathe in and pull life energy from the ground into your body. As you breathe out push life energy from your right hand towards your left hand through your partner's shoulder joint.

Breathe in and push the life energy back from the left towards your right hand and at the same time pull it with your right hand against your left hand. As you continue to breathe in and out move the life energy through your partner's shoulder back and forth from one hand to the other, one always pushing and the other pulling. Feel the life energy flow arrive at the pulling hand and continue for as long as you get the impression that there is no more resistance in the tissue of your partner's shoulder and that the flow has definitely increased. At this stage your partner may also be able to sense the flow of life energy as well and in addition will probably feel a comfortable sensation of warmth not only on the surface but all also throughout his whole shoulder joint.

When you scan your partner's shoulder once again record all the changes which you are able to find and check with your partner if they feel any differences comparing the left and right shoulder. Discuss the results and find out if there are any correlations between the results of your scan on one hand and your partner's impressions on the other.

Exercise 2: Flushing an Intervertebral Disc

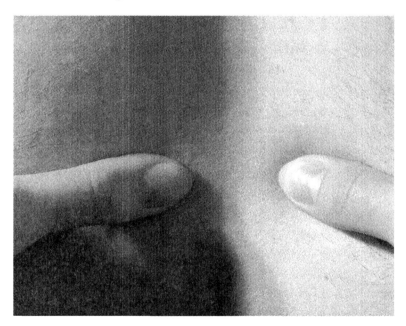

Sit behind your partner. Find the spinal process of the fifth lumbar vertebra and place both your thumbs, one on each side, over the area where your fifth lumbar vertebra meets the sacrum. You will find this position directly below on both sides of the spine.

Now breathe in and draw life energy from the ground into your body. As you breathe out, push life energy from your right thumb towards your left thumb through the intervertebral disc between the fifth lumbar vertebra and the sacrum. Breathe in and push the energy back from the left towards your right thumb and at the same time pull the energy back with your right thumb towards your left thumb. Continue to breathe in this way, moving the life energy through your partner's disc from one thumb to the other, one pushing and the other pulling. Feel the flow arriving on the pulling thumb. Continue this for as long as you get the impression that there is no more resistance and the flow has increased.

Ask your partner if they can feel a sensation of warmth; inquire whether this sensation stays local or whether it radiates into the legs.

You have been successful with this exercise when you have an impression of a change occurring within the energy field and when your partner has also been able at the same time to feel clearly any sensation there.

Dissolving

Once you have mastered some basic techniques of the directed care method which can be used to treat spine problems, you are ready to learn some more advanced techniques. These can then be used to treat chronic or persistent back problems. One can compare these problems to stains which remain on your clothes after you have washed them. Such "stains" which exist within the life energy field even after you have flushed a specific area, will always have a very destructive effect on the affected tissue. These kinds of tenacious stains in the life energy field or aura can occur on a physical level as an inflammatory process, or in the form of a low metabolism rate in the cells, or even as a pathological growth of cells like cancer within a particular area in the body.

You will need to use special techniques to dissolve continuous destructive blockages in such areas. Once the flow of life energy is restored, it will revitalize the affected tissue and in the best case lead to a self healing process of the physical body or at least help prevent the situation from becoming worse. When treating spine problems, the technique of dissolving is mainly used to treat very small areas and therefore can be done only with your fingertips.

For the following exercise you will need to work with someone who is older and probably suffering from some chronic spine problems. If you follow the instructions in this exercise precisely you cannot do any harm to your partner you may help to ease some of their problems.

Exercise: Dissolving a Blockage

Sit behind your partner and gently lay both of your thumbs or your thumb and forefinger in the little hollow under the dorsal process of the fifth lumbar vertebra. Flush the area where the fifth lumbar vertebra and the sacrum meet each other until you feel an increased and smoother flow of life energy. Your partner will eventually recognize this as a feeling of warmth.

If this works without any problem move up to the space between the fourth and the fifth lumbar vertebra and once again flush the area there.

Repeat this technique all the way up the whole spine until you reach a spot where it is very difficult or even impossible to achieve an increased flow. It may occur in the first area where you laid your fingers on – between the fifth lumbar vertebra and the sacrum – or it may occur somewhere higher up on the spine.

When you find such a spot, adjust your perception to get a clear impression of the characteristics of the blockage. Does it have a hotter and more aggressive character or do you feel any kind of stagnation? Trust your instincts because it is always your first impressions which provide the best information. The more you begin to question your perception the more difficult it will be for you to get a clear picture.

First dissolve the blockage by pushing life energy through your fingertips into the area and then pulling it out again. Repeat this pumping movement of life energy until you can feel a change in the field of the area you are working on. Now begin to flush the area. If you have been successful in dissolving the blockage you will now be able to perceive a smoother and increased flow of life energy. If you do not, then begin once again to use the dissolving technique.

Discuss with your partner to see if he feels any changes within his back for example is there less pain and are his movements more flexible?

Light Waves and Sound Waves

Hands-on healing works in two ways. One way is to influence the body of light by changing the electromagnetic information stored there, and the second way is by penetrating the tissue and treating it directly on a cellular level with life energy. In some cases, influencing the light body may lead to a spontaneous reaction within the physical body which may result in fewer symptoms, and in the best case scenario, your client may be instantly healed. Unfortunately there are a lot of uncertainties in such a process, especially in cases where there is severe damaged tissue, such as a prolapsed disc. It is extremely difficult to achieve a success in such acute cases by only rewriting the electromagnetic information within the affected area. Your client may feel some short- term pain relief but this will not last long and he will leave in the same condition he was in when he first came to you.

The reason why changes of information within the electromagnetic field of life energy cannot bring about the desired healing is due to the fact that severely damaged tissue will change back and overwrite again and again whatever changes you have implemented within the body of light. We therefore have to look for another way to finally solve this problem in order to bring about a more satisfying result. It requires a technique which is able to achieve changes directly within the tissue and this means finding a way to penetrate the physical body.

Light will not be able to do that as it will reflect on any physical surface. Sound, on the other hand, can penetrate even massive walls of concrete. Sound also possesses the characteristic of being able to stimulate cell growth and metabolism. This has often been proven by the fact that plants, for example, show a positive response and have an increased growth when music is played for them.

As healers we have to take advantage of such a phenomenon. In order to extend the sound waves they need to be on a high frequency. You can do this by contracting your skeletal muscles as much as possible and transmitting these waves through your hands into your client's body directly to the specific area you like to work on.

The use of sound waves in hands-on healing provides a direct stimulation of tissue on a cellular level which will show amazing results when it is applied on any degenerative changes within the spine. In such cases, sound wave techniques should be applied first, after which the affected areas can also be treated with light waves so as to achieve the best possible results. For the following exercise you will need a partner.

Exercise: Creating Sound Waves within a Large Area

Lay your right hand on the back of your partner's right shoulder joint and your left hand on its front. Breathe in and take life energy from the ground into your body. As you breathe out, push it from your right hand towards your left hand through your partner's shoulder joint. Breathe in and push the life energy back from the left hand towards your right hand and at the same time pull it with your right hand from your left hand. As you continue to breathe in this way, move the life energy through your partner's shoulder from one hand to the other, using one hand pushing and the other pulling. Feel the flow arriving at the pulling hand and continue until you get the impression that there is no more resistance from the tissue of your partner's shoulder and there is a definite increase in the flow of the life energy.

Ask your partner to remember the sensations they feel while you are treating them so that they can later compare it to the sensations they feel when you are using sound waves.

Keep the same position as before. Now push life energy with both hands into your partner's shoulder. At the same time, contract all the muscles within your arms and hands as much as possible. You will soon find your arms and hands starting to vibrate. Keep this vibration for as long as you can, then stop.

Compare the results. Does your partner feel any difference now? Do they feel any heat inside the shoulder? Do they feel the vibration not only on the surface of their shoulder but deep within the joint? Do they describe the sensation as a vibrating heat in the shoulder joint? If the answers to these questions are a clear yes, then you have done a good job. If not, try again after a while and do it as often as possible until you achieve the desired results.

Exercise: Creating Sound Waves within a Small Area
Sit behind your partner and gently lay either both your thumbs or the thumb and the forefinger in the little hollow under the dorsal process of the fifth lumbar vertebra. Breathe in and take life energy from the ground into your body. As you breathe out, push it from your thumbs into the intervertebral disc between the fifth lumbar vertebra and the sacrum.

Contract all the muscles in your arms and thumbs. When you feel your thumbs vibrating a little, keep this vibration for as long as possible.

Ask your partner whether they felt a vibrating sensation of heat inside the spine on the area you were working on. If not, try once more until your partner is able to feel this and you achieved the desired result.

Changing Frequencies
Different frequencies within the field of life energy are defined by different colors of light and these seven colors of the rainbow have great significance for healers. According to the chakra system, each color represents a specific quality of life energy. When a healer is able to produce different colors and transmit them into the client's light body, they can influence the quality – which is the brightness and clearness – of the aura or life energy field, and it is also then possible for the healer to change the colors on specific areas. Any change of quality within the light body will have a direct influence on the tissue. For example, pain caused by an inflammation may occur as a dark red area within the aura. When a healer changes this color, which represents a destructive process

on a specific area of the body, the inflammation will disappear as soon as the color changes and the tissue regenerates.

It is therefore necessary to be able to sense the different frequencies or colors either kinaesthetically or visually, or ideally in both ways. Besides this, an experienced healer should be able to transform the life energy they absorb from earth into the colors of the rainbow so that they can use them separately and be able to direct it to wherever it is needed.

Scientific evidence for this phenomenon of changing frequencies or colors was provided by the *Rolf Study* done at the University of California Los Angeles. *Dr Valerie V. Hunt*, a physician, together with the clairvoyant and internationally recognized aura reader and healer *Rosalyn L. Bruyere,* noted that the traditional teachings of the chakras and its colors occurring within the aura corresponded to the results of the electronic apparatus used to measure the field of life energy of the test persons.

In this experiment, electrodes were fixed to the areas of the major chakras and some of the meridian points of the test persons. These test subjects received a number of *Rolfing* treatments (*Rolfing* is a kind of deep connective tissue massage). Whatever the test person experienced during the treatment was measured and recorded by different electronic instruments while the aura reader simultaneously recorded her observations on tape. The results of the electronic measurements and the observations of the aura reader corresponded closely to each other. The more Rolfing treatments the test persons had, the more changes of colors or frequencies were recorded both by the aura reader and the instruments. This implies that in hands-on healing it is possible to intentionally change the frequencies within the field of life energy or colors of the aura.

The chakras of the test persons often showed colors which were the same as those assigned by traditional literature. Traditionally the first chakra on the pelvis area is red and the second chakra situated at the lower part of the stomach is orange. The third chakra which is around the spleen area is yellow, and the fourth chakra covering the chest is green. The fifth chakra, which is on the throat, is light blue, and the sixth chakra on the area around the forehead, is indigo purple. Finally, the seventh chakra which is situated on the top of the head, was white (in traditional teachings of the aura it is said to be either violet or white). Another interesting observation made by the Rolf Study was that the different colors assigned to each chakra did not remain static but were found to be floating up and down in different areas of the body. When any work was done on one chakra it automatically influenced all the others.

The following exercise will show how you can produce different colors of light. Once you have acquired this skill by practicing this exercise for a while you will be able to use it easily in a healing session without needing any other prior preparation.

Exercise: Transforming Life Energy into Separate Colors

Stand on the floor with your feet shoulder width apart and ensure that your weight is equally distributed on both your feet. Be aware that your weight is also equally distributed across the soles of your feet. Your heels, toes, the balls of your feet and the arches should have equal pressure on the floor.

Bend the knees so that they are in line with your toes. Move your pelvis forward a little and bring your chin to your throat to straighten and stretch all your vertebrae. Imagine a string running straight from the top of your head right through your body down to the perineum and from there to the floor. Align your standing position along this imaginary string without building any tension.

Keep the shoulders and neck relaxed. As you breathe in, lift your arms in front of your body to your shoulders. Focus on the balls of your feet and think of them as being suction cups. Intentionally let life energy flow from the ground into your first chakra, which is the area around your genitals and your sacrum.

Breathe out and push life energy which has been transformed to red through your arms as you bend your palms up and straighten your arms forward. Slowly bring your arms back to the starting position. Repeat these movements until you feel a clear sensation of prickling heat on your palms and fingers.

Bring your hands to the belly button and turn them so that your palms are facing each other at a distance of approximately eighteen inches or half a meter apart. Now send red life energy intentionally from your right palm towards your left. If you feel a prickling sensation of heat there you are now able to directly transmit pure red light.

Breathe in again and bring your arms in front of your body up to your shoulders. Let life energy flow from the ground into your second chakra, which covers your intestines. Breathe out and push life energy transformed to orange, from your second chakra to your arms, as your bend your palms up and straighten your arms forward.

Bring your arms slowly back to the starting position. Repeat these movements until you feel a clear sensation of a "liquid" like warmth on your palms.

Raise your hands to your belly button and turn them so that your left palm is under your right palm at a distance of approximately twelve inches or thirty centimetres apart. Now intentionally send orange life energy from your right palm to your left. If you feel a warm "liquid" flowing over your left hand, you are able to directly transmit pure orange light.

Breathe in again and lift your arms in front of your body up to your shoulders. Let life energy flow from the ground into your third chakra, which is found below the sternum with its centre slightly to the left side of the body. It covers the liver, spleen, pancreas and the kidneys. Breathe out and push life energy transformed to yellow from there through your arms, as your bend your palms up and straighten your arms forward.

Slowly bring your arms back to the starting position. Repeat these movements until you can feel a clear sensation of a "cool air" on your palms.

Raise your hands to your belly button and turn them so that your left palm is under your right palm at a distance of approximately twelve inches or thirty centimetres apart. Now intentionally send yellow life energy from your right palm towards your left palm. If you feel "cool air" flowing over your left hand you are able to directly transmit pure yellow light.

Breathe in again and lift your arms in front of your body up to your shoulders. Bring the life energy from the ground into your fourth chakra, which covers your chest area. Breathe out and push life energy transformed to green from there through your arms, as you bend your palms up and straighten your arms forward. Repeat these movements until you feel a clear sensation of a "heavy feeling" on your palms and fingers.

Now intentionally send green life energy from the fourth chakra into your hands. If you feel how full or "heavy" they have become, you are able to directly transmit pure green light.

Breathe in again and lift your arms in front of your body up to your shoulders. Let life energy flow from the ground into your fifth chakra, which covers your throat. Breathe out and push life energy transformed to bright blue from there through your arms, as you bend your palms up and straighten your arms forward. Repeat these movements until you feel a clear sensation of a "cold flow" on your fingertips.

Now intentionally send bright blue light from the fifth chakra into your hands, and if you feel a "cold flow" around your finger tips you are able to directly transmit pure bright blue light.

Breathe in once more and lift your arms in front of your body up to your shoulders. Let life energy flow from the ground into your sixth chakra, which you can be found around your forehead. Breathe out and push life energy transformed to purple light from there through your arms as you bend your palms up and straighten your arms forward. Repeat these movements until you can feel a clear sensation of a "warm flow" on your fingertips.

Intentionally send this purple light from the sixth chakra into your hands. If you feel a "warm flow" around your finger tips you are able to directly transmit pure violet light.

You can practice all these together with a partner. This will give you an added advantage of providing you with instant feedback. The first thing you should do is to transform life energy to any color you want. Then transmit the pure color you created into the palms of your partner without touching him. Ask your partner if they are able to feel the different sensations as described above.

CHAPTER10

Specific Hands on Healing Techniques

for the Spine

If you have followed and practiced all the exercises and techniques suggested in the previous chapters you may have acquired all the basic tools necessary to use hands-on healing successfully. In this chapter you will learn specific techniques to treat different back problems. The techniques in this chapter can be used by professional therapists to widen their range of tools and also by those who want to use them to treat relatives and friends suffering from spine problems to help them improve their quality of life.

As a beginner you should focus especially on the technique called *Reawakening Snake Power* to increase the general level of life energy and provide immediate pain relief.

In any hands-on healing sessions, regardless of whether you are a professional or not, you first have to learn how to make a proper assessment of the person you want to treat. This assessment is an essential precondition so that you can use the most appropriate techniques on the right area and then check later to see what changes your treatment may have caused in your client's life energy field. Once you are more experienced you will know from your recorded assessments the most suitable techniques to use, as you will be more aware of the effects you can achieve when you apply a particular technique.

Assessment
Let us look now at some of the factors you as a healer have to consider when a client comes to you for treatment. As soon as

your client walks in, observe closely the way they walk and look at them from all angles, from the front as well as the back. Within this "obvious" appearance you will be able to find a lot of important information about your client that may go unnnoticed by those who only look superficially at a person. Many people don't tell you enough to really enable you to understand the causes of their problems. This is because many people are not used to talking openly about themselves and their problems. Another major issue is that there is a big difference between the way people perceive themselves and a more objective version of reality.

The basic information about whether a client needs a relaxing or an energizing treatment should become clear to you a soon as they first step into your treatment room. Observe the way the client walks. Are their movements stiff or flexible? Does he stomp in heavily on his heels or is his walk springy? Notice how your client comes into the room. Does he rush in, or does he have a more relaxed approach? Or does he stagger in rather than walk? Look closely at the person; look at their posture when they stand in front of you. Is their posture upright (chest out, stomach in)? Are their shoulders on an equal height? Is the client's posture more of a question mark?

Do they have bright eyes which promise vitality and humour or do the eyes look dull, as if they are fading away like a faint dim light? Do they speak up or do they whisper to you? As you mentally record all these details about your client you will have a lot of information about their whole personality even before they have greeted you.

The next thing you need to do is to ask your client what specific spine problems they are suffering from. It is even better if a client is able to bring you the results of an X-ray or MRI exami-nation. In cases where the client reports some feelings of numbness, tickling sensations radiating into the extremities, or is experiencing a partial paralysis in the limbs, the client should definitely be medically diagnosed in order to avoid further complications. There are some forms of prolapsed disc which require immediate surgery and for your client's safety this should be clarified first. In any case, a medical diagnosis is the best feedback you can have to check the results of your own assessments.

Lower Back Assessment

If your client is suffering from lower back pain ask him to lie on his stomach on a massage couch. If you have no massage couch, something similar like a big dining table would do, or you may ask your client to lie on the floor. Support your client's pelvis by placing a flat cushion there so that the lumbar vertebra is not overstretched. Support his ankles with a rolled up blanket.

Lay the middle finger of your right or left hand – whichever one you prefer – on the end of your client's coccyx and your thumb on the upper end of his sacrum.

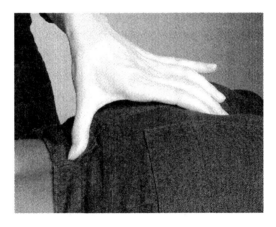

Gently let life energy flow into the coccyx, then in the sacrum and then through each single lumbar vertebra up to the 12th thoracic vertebra where the chest ends. While you do this follow the movement of life energy as closely as possible, kinaesthetically as well as visually.

The flow of life energy may be interrupted, stopped or deflected at some point. Go there and put your first and second finger on that spot. First you may recognize increased muscular tension there. Gently push life energy deeper into the tissue so that you can reach the cartilage and osseous structures as well.

The first noticeable symptom is any kind of interruption or deflection of the diagnostic flow you have initiated. Record the specific area where you have found this interruption and this is where you will later begin to change the energy field. Check whether the area you have identified is in any way connected to the symptoms described by your client. If the client complains of radiating symptoms in his legs, check if the area you have identified corresponds to the segmental origin of that symptom.
(You can find a segmental chart in the section on *Segmental Pain Relief*).

Now analyze the spot and decide how you want to treat it. First you have to make a distinction between the two kinds of imbalances which can occur in the affected area.

The first one would be a state where there is an overabundance of life energy. This occurs when there is congestion of life energy. This may manifest itself as an inflammatory process on the physical level. Overabundance of life energy can be felt as a kind of swelling because there is hardly any flow within the affected area. In such a spot the life energy would have a high density and the consistency would be sluggish and not as "elastic" as it should be. A thermal characteristic of this overabundance ranges from an increased warmth to heat which sometimes feels like needle pricks.

The other extreme characteristic you may find is "emptiness". There is a lack of life energy which may in the worst case be felt as if there is a "hole". You may find nothing there. Otherwise you may experience the field as being very thin at the affected area and as a thermal sensation it may range from cool to cold.

Once you have finished your analysis you have to decide which kind of technique you want to use. For example, if there is an overabundance you can use the *Dissolving* technique while in a case of emptiness you may choose *Flushing*.

After you have treated the affected area, if your client still has any other symptoms, start again from the beginning and look for other areas of imbalance.

Cervical and Thoracic Assessment

In cases where your client complains that he is unable to move and has pain around the neck and shoulder areas, ask him to lie on his back on a massage couch. If you do not have a massage couch then use something similar like a big dining table, or you may ask your client to lie on the floor. Place a rolled up blanket under his knees for support.

Sit behind your client and hold the back of his head on your palms so that your fingertips are at the base of his head and your client's ears are between your thumbs and your first finger.

Gently pull life energy from your client's spine until you can clearly feel his chest, shoulders and neck. The more you know about the anatomy of this area, the easier it will be to recognize a blockage or deflection when it occurs there. To achieve the

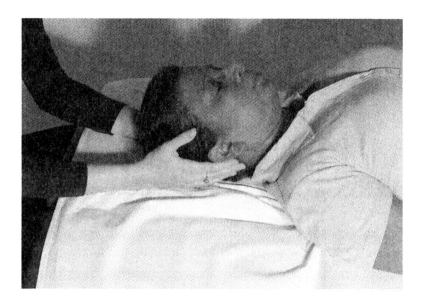

best results you should be familiar with the neck and shoulder exercises mentioned in Chapter Six. When you practice these exercises you develop a very advanced level of self awareness which enables you to perceive imbalances within your client's body as if it is reflected within your own. Whenever you have an intuition that there is something not quite in balance you can also check and compare that to the same structures within your own body.

It often happens that the pain your client describes does not have its origin in the area where it is felt by him. Analyze the whole thoracic and cervical spine vertebra by vertebra and see if you can find areas where there is an overabundance or emptiness which you recognize by the same characteristics that have been described when we mentioned the lumbar area. See if you can find a connection between the painful areas and their segmental origins that you have found. (Refer to the segmental chart).

Be aware that an overabundance of life energy usually goes hand in hand with an increased muscular tension and a restriction in movement and that emptiness occurs mainly where the tissues are weak.

Now decide on the kind of technique you want to use. After you have sorted out one affected area, if you still see any other kinds of symptoms, start again from the beginning and look for other areas of imbalance that still need to be treated.

Reawakening the Snake Power

The name *"Snake Power"* seems to be rather daunting. It is nothing else but a synonym for life energy that ascends through the spine, which is the main channel within the human body. There is therefore no need to be afraid of receiving a treatment in which the *"Snake Power"* is reawakened. This treatment improves the quality of life. For example, it is a technique that those who care for the elderly can do to bring comfort to their patients, it is a way that couples can offer support to each other, and friends can help other friends who are suffering from back problems. This technique is so easy to use and it also enriches the work of professional therapists.

Whenever back problems occur it is usually related to a deflection of the flow of life energy from the pelvis region to the head. This weakens the main chakras which transform life energy into different frequencies so that they are unable to fulfil their specific functions. When the Chakras spin out of sync or change their original position it results in physical and psychological problems.

By using this method to treat someone you will be able to relax, reenergize and invigorate this person. They will certainly have less back pain after this treatment. However, they may not remain totally pain free for very long, especially if they have a long history of severe back problems. The *Reawakening the Snake Power* technique can be used as a preparation for treating special problems such as a prolapsed disc. Used at the end of a massage it will enhance the effects and the results will be even more remarkable. Whichever way you use this technique it will improve the flow of life energy through the spine. The intervertebral discs that act as a kind of "battery" for life energy will also be recharged.

This treatment has many advantages on a psychological level. First of all it creates a state of deep relaxation which reduces stress considerably as many back problems originate from emotions such as anxiety. As soon as stress and emotionally related tensions embedded in the deepest muscular layers are dissolved, it will automatically change the emotional state of your client. This includes any old traumas which are still stored within the muscular tissue. You can also support any psychotherapeutic work that your client is undergoing as they will have the opportunity to release emotional traumas which had been hidden within the physical body as well as in the body of light. Sometimes the emotional release caused by this treatment may make your client cry. Do not be afraid if this happens, as a healer you are there to to provide a safe and supportive atmosphere where your client is able to rediscover and experience emotions which may have been suppressed for a long time.

You can treat your client in one of the following positions that feels most comfortable:

They can lay on their stomach – in this case support their pelvis with a flat cushion and their ankles with a rolled up blanket. If your client decides to lie on their side, you should put a small cushion between their knees for comfort. For both these positions you need a massage couch or a big dining table. The third and most common possibility is to ask your client to sit in front of you with their back facing you.

In all these three positions you can use both your thumbs or just the thumb and the index finger of the hand you prefer. Working with one hand is highly recommended if the client is on their stomach or their side. When your client sits in front of you it is better to use both your thumbs.

You always start on the sacrum. There are eight little holes – four on each side. Feel for the first bottom pair and begin there.

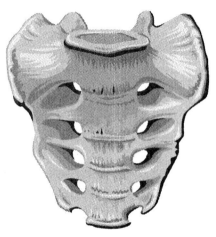

Gently place your thumbs there while you rest your hands on your client's buttocks. As you breathe in take life energy from the ground through the soles of your feet, into your body. As you breathe out, intentionally push life energy through your thumbs into the first pair of holes on your client's sacrum. If you are working with only one hand because your client is lying on their stomach or their side, you can put your thumb and your index finger on the holes which are on either side of the sacrum. Place your other hand on the upper part of your client's chest.

Now take life energy from the ground into your body as you breathe in and as you breathe out intentionally push life energy through your thumb and your index finger into the bottom pair of holes within your client's sacrum.

Now put both of your thumbs, or if you are using only one

hand your thumb and index finger, on the next pair of holes, and again push life energy into them. Repeat this until you reach the upper pair of holes.

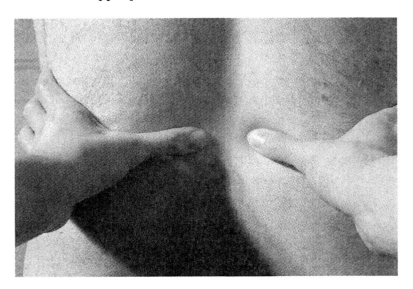

After you have finished doing this, continue to work on the area above the sacrum. This is where you will find a tiny depression between the sacrum and the fifth lumbar vertebra on each side of the spine. Do not use too much pressure. Lay both of your thumbs or your thumb and index finger gently there. You will find a similar depression between all the vertebrae as you move up the spine. Put your thumbs there, or your thumb and index finger if you are using only one hand, and begin to push life energy in.

As you reach the small pair of depressions between the first lumbar and the twelfth thoracic vertebra, and if you are only working with one hand then place your second hand on the back of your client's head. If you are using both your thumbs, place the rest of your hand very lightly on your client's back as before.

Continue pushing life energy into the area between the vertebrae where the vertebral discs are situated until you reach the *Prominens* –the protruding seventh cervical vertebra. Now if you are using both your thumbs, touch your client only with these and spread the rest of your hands away from his neck. If you are using only one hand keep your second hand on the back of your client's head.

When you arrive the base of the head, finish the treatment by placing one of your hands on your client's sacrum and the other on the back of his head. Once again push life energy through both your hands into your client's body.

Then remove your hands and let your client rest for a little while. Complete this treatment by offering him a glass of water.

Lower Back Technique

The lower back area includes the sacrum and the lumbar spine. These areas are easily affected by degenerative changes. The probability of having a prolapsed disc is high, especially between the fifth lumbar vertebra and the sacrum. Increased muscular tension in the lumbar area can also cause a change of the spine's curvature which can result in a lot of pain there. When there is increased muscular tension within the buttocks and the psoas muscle it will also lead to a restriction in the flexibility of the pelvis and will later affect the whole spine. A physically inflexible pelvis will change the rhythm of movement along the whole spine and cause tension in all the upper parts of the spine.

The kundalini or "coiled up snake" symbolized in the yogic tradition, is a symbol of life energy and represents the spiritual potential inherent in everyone. In the physical body the origin of the kundalini energy is in the pelvis, particularly at the sacrum. One needs to grow spiritually in order to tap into all the abilities one can achieve as a human being. This is done by raising the kundalini along the spine into the brain. A pelvis that is inflexible will withhold the spiritual aspect of life energy, making it impossible for the kundalini to rise. In this case it will never really be possible for someone to achieve any kind of tangible spiritual development.

This lower back treatment is designed to make the pelvis and lumbar area more flexible in order to prevent degenerative changes as well as being a technique to provide pain relief there. It can be used on its own or as an additional technique to relax a larger area around affected spots when you are treating a prolapsed disc or any other specific problem in the lower back area. If you use this technique soon after a massage or any kind of physiotherapy you will have much better results because you are reinforcing the treatment in both physical body and the body of light.

For treating your client you will need a massage couch or something similar like a big dining table. You can also do it on the floor but this is not recommended because as a healer you may create problems for your own back if you are working in such an uncomfortable position all the time. Ask your client if they prefer to lie on their stomach or on their side. If they prefer to lie on their stomach then support their pelvis with a flat cushion and the ankles with a rolled up blanket. If your client prefers to lie on their side then they should lie on the side that has less problems or pain, and a flat cushion should be placed between their knees.

Place the fingers of both your hands except your thumbs in the very middle of your client's sacrum. As you breathe in take life energy from the ground through your soles of your feet into your body. As you breathe out push it through your fingertips into your client's sacrum. Use the pumping technique of life energy by breathing in and out until you feel a strong flow of life energy from the ground through your body into your client. This flow should be independent of the conscious effort you make to begin with.

Continue to push life energy into the sacrum of your client until you can clearly sense a shift within this area. Such a shift may occur as an increased warmth, an "easier" quality of flow or an "enlarged" space which can be sensed kinaesthetically around the sacrum area. Visually you may perceive a change of color there if you have developed your perception skills this far.

Now move your fingertips up and place them on the spinal processes of the fifth, the fourth and the third lumbar vertebra. Again push life energy into this area until you can feel a shift of life energy. This will physically appear as having less tension in the muscles along the spine.

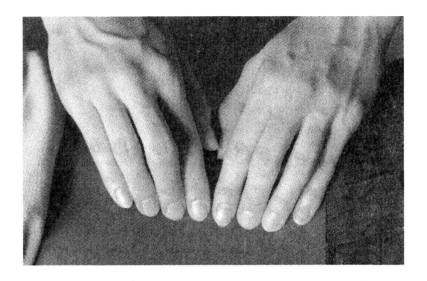

Move your fingers up a notch and place the fingertips on the spinal processes of the third, second and first lumbar vertebra. Push life energy in until you feel a shift.

Now ask your client to sit up with both their legs hanging over one side of the couch. Sit behind him and place your hands on your client's back on the area where his kidneys are.

Push life energy by distributing it equally into both kidneys. This requires you to be totally aware of the flow of life energy as it should be equally strong in both your hands.

When you experience a shift of life energy in your clients kidneys close up the treatment by offering your client a glass of water.

Thoracic Technique

This technique can be used to treat a number of back problems because it provides a general release of tension particularly in the thoracic area. Pain which persists either physically or emotionally over a longer period of time will lead to a state where the life energy becomes permanently blocked. By using this technique, which has its starting point in the middle of the chest, all blockages can be easily dissolved.

This is also a very good treatment to improve the breathing capacity of the lungs when it is restricted because of different conditions such as asthma, allergies, bronchitis caused by an infection, or even lung cancer. Whenever breathing problems occur they lead to an increased muscular tension between the scapulae and parts of the shoulder area. This causes inflexibility of the lower ribs and restricts the range of the movement of the diaphragm.

Breathing problems and increased muscular tension within the chest area may be caused by some kind of emotional problems. A "broken heart" is the result of a number of emotional traumas and to avoid further grief people often unconsciously close up physically by reducing the intensity of their breathing. Breathing deeply and feeling oneself intensely – on a physical as well as on an emotional level – always goes hand in hand. When you release the tension within your client's thoracic spine and chest it may lead to the release of past emotional traumas that have been suppressed in the subconscious. This may come in the form of an emotional release and tears. By applying this treatment you heal emotional scars that have been etched into your client's light body. Seen in this way, the *Thoracic Treatment* definitely provides a strong support to your client when they are undergoing psychotherapy because they will be able to access traumas hidden within the unconsciousness more easily.

For this technique use either a massage couch, a big dining table or if neither is available, ask your client to lie directly on the floor. It is better not to use this position regularly because of the problems it may cause to the healer's back. Uncomfortable body postures will restrict the healer's work.

Ask your client to lie on their right side to ensure that their weight is not pressing against the heart. Support your client's head with a pillow and place a flat cushion between their knees for comfort.

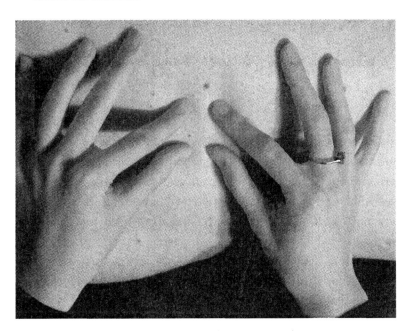

Place the index fingers and thumbs of both your hands between the sixth and the seventh thoracic vertebra. To find this spot you can count down the spinal processes of the thoracic vertebrae or you can use as a point of reference the spot which is directly opposite the middle of the sternum.

Now with your index fingers and thumbs pull the life energy apart and extend the space between the two vertebrae. Once you can perceive a "dissolving" effect on this area, move your hands apart until your thumbs and index fingers are placed on the upper end between the fifth and the sixth and with the lower hand between the seventh and the eight thoracic vertebras. Continue pulling life energy apart within this larger area until you are able to feel the "dissolving" effect.

Then move your index fingers and both your thumbs to the next pair of vertebras and pull life energy apart as you had done before. Repeat this process along the whole thoracic spine while observing closely the reaction of your client to your treatment. It should always be a relaxing and pleasant experience as they feel the expansion as a kind of warm flowing energy along their spine.

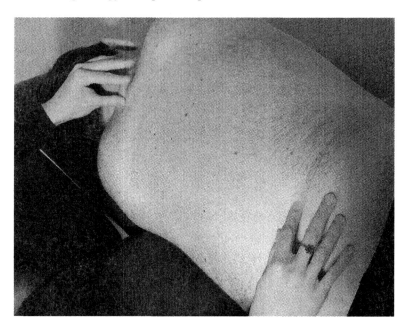

When you have reached the seventh cervical vertebra with your left hand and the first lumbar vertebra with your right hand, continue pulling and expanding along the cervical and lumbar spine.

Continue to do this until you reach the base of the head with one hand and the sacrum with the other.

Finish the treatment by offering your client a glass of water.

Neck and Shoulder Technique

A stiff and painful neck, problems bending and turning the neck, and headaches related to increased muscular tension within the neck and shoulder areas, are common ailments afflicting a large number of office workers and many individuals who are permanently under stress. People suffering from neck problems always have a significant lack of awareness of their own physical condition. Neck problems may also be the result of a person's inability to communicate and express their thoughts through speech.

The neck and shoulder treatment explained below alleviates a wide range of neck related problems. It can also help to increase self awareness and support a person's spiritual growth. This technique can be used separately or to complement a specific treatment, for example to treat a prolapsed disc in the cervical spine.

The neck and shoulder technique is also easy to integrate within a massage or physiotherapy session where it will further enhance the benefits of the treatment. The duration of this treatment is between fifteen and twenty minutes.

Ask your client to lie on their back on a massage couch, if this is not available on a big dining table or if need be on the floor. Support their knees with a rolled up blanket. Sit behind their head.

Place the fingertips of both of your middle fingers gently on each side of the *Prominens* which is the protruding seventh cervical vertebra. This is a very delicate area where an important neuronal plexus is situated. Even the slightest touch which becomes too intense or too strong a penetration of life energy may cause tingling or paralysing sensations radiating into your client's arms, especially if there are any degenerative changes found in the spine in this area. Be constantly aware of

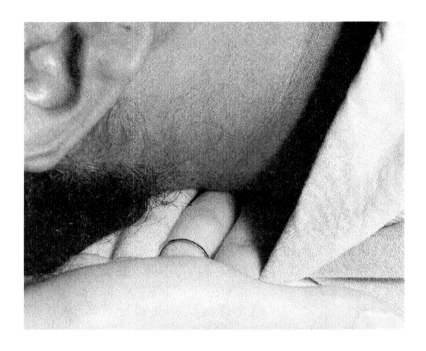

this and ask your client to immediately tell you of any unusual sensations so that you can adjust the treatment accordingly.

Begin very gently by using the "dissolving" technique, increasing the intensity in accordance to the feedback you get from your client until you can clearly perceive a shift of life energy in this area.

On a physical level it will reduce muscular tension and you will definitely experience an increased flow as well as an "enlarged" space in the field of life energy. Visually you may also perceive a brighter and clearer light there. Your client may describe this as a warm flow through his arms and in case there had been some painful sensations radiating from this area into the arms they should be gone now.

Move your fingertips up and place them between the seventh

and the sixth cervical vertebra. Once again apply the dissolving technique until you feel a shift. Continue this along the whole cervical spine. Between the third and the fourth vertebra you will again reach a very delicate spot which you should be particularly aware of.

Once you reached the base of your client's head, take the back of their head into your palms. Ensure that your fingertips are lying at the base of the head and your client's ears are between your thumbs and your first finger. By holding your client's head in this position you are creating a flow through their whole spine. Check with your client to see if they can clearly perceive the sensation of a warm flow through the spine.

When you receive a positive feedback finish the session by offering them a glass of water.

Segmental Pain Relief

Every nerve which leaves the spine between two particular vertebrae supports a specific area of the body. For example the hip area, the lower front side of the upper leg and the inner parts of the knee are supported by a nerve which has its origin between the third and the fourth lumbar vertebra. Such areas that are connected by one spinal nerve are called segments. Let us look at one particular segment, for example the L3 which is the third lumbar vertebra. Whenever you want to successfully relieve pain which is radiating into your client's extremities then you have to treat the problem at the place of its origin: a narrowed nerve root. This may have been caused by an increased tension of the autochthon muscles, degenerative changes of the spine, prolapsed discs or cancer.

Ask your client to pinpoint the exact spot the pain radiates to in his arms or legs. Compare the results to the segmental chart

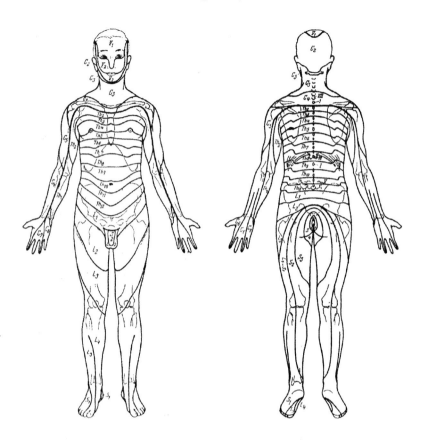

below and you will know exactly where to find the origin of this problem. The problem is always a narrowed space around a spinal nerve root. This implies that there has been an accumulation of too much life energy there.

To treat the lower back and the thoracic area, ask your client to lie on their stomach or on their side, according to their preference. If your client chooses to lie on their stomach, support the pelvis with a flat cushion. If they prefer to lie on their side, make sure that they are on the side which has less pain or no symptoms.

When you are treating your client's neck, ask them to lie on their back. You can improve your results by gently stretching your client's neck with one hand and dissolving a congested area with the fingers of your other hand.

Dissolve the congestion of life energy with your fingers but always be aware that you are working on a very delicate area. Be gentle with your touch and ask your client to immediately mention if they feels any increase in pain. If this is the case, reduce the intensity of the physical touch and the flow of life energy. Whenever there is more pain you have to reduce the "pushing" sequences and use more of the "pulling" technique. It is also advantageous in such cases to change the color to a higher and cooler frequency, either a light blue or indigo. Once you have found the appropriate balance between the "pushing" and "pulling" your client will report an immediate relief of pain. You can use this technique to treat any irritated nerve root all over the spine which causes problems.

Degenerative Changes

There are two ways to treat degenerative changes within the spine with the hands-on healing method. One is to create changes within the body of light and the other is to directly penetrate the physical body with sound waves to achieve changes on a cellular level. You get the best results by combining these two methods.

If we accept the idea that the human body is a holistic functional unit and that there are often underlying emotional or mental reasons which in the end lead to physical damages then it is clear that the combination of light and sound waves used in a treatment session will heal the symptoms and the causes simulta-neously.

To achieve the best results you should also treat a degenerative change using one of the more general techniques which have been mentioned earlier. This ensures that your client is more relaxed and their overall feeling of wellbeing is improved.

The following treatment session described below is for a client suffering from severe degenerative changes within her lumbar vertebra. As always use this example of the treatment only as a guideline and vary it according to the needs of client. You can apply the concepts and ideas introduced to you in this section on any other area of the spine by following this guideline:

1. An Assessment
2. General Relaxation
3. Pain Relief
4. Tissue Restructuring
5. Stabilizing

An Outline of a Session to Treat Degenerative Changes within the Lumbar Spine

Assessment
The client is around 75 years old and suffers from severe back pain which radiates into her legs. This has considerably reduced her ability to move around and has affected the quality of her day-to-day life. The radiologist report states that she is suffering from *Spondylisis* and *Ostoephytes* which cause the narrowing of the nerve root particularly between the third and the fourth lumbar vertebra and also between the fifth lumbar and the first sacral vertebra.

Treatment
Firstly, place your thumb and your index finger both at the lower end of the coccyx and the upper end of the sacrum. Gently push life energy along your client's spine. If you do not sense any imbalance in the areas develop your perceptions by scanning the areas identified by the radiologist's report. You will soon learn to distinguish between a balanced and imbalanced flow of life energy.

1. Use the *Lower Back Treatment* to relax the entire lower back of your client.

2. You can successfully relief local and radiating pain by using the *Segmental Pain Relief* technique.

3. As soon as you dissolve a local blockage in the client's body of light you have to "recharge" the exhausted and degenerated tissue. Use sound waves on the frequency of red light to penetrate as deeply as possible the whole area from the skin into the bone and cartilage of a vertebra.

4. Ask your client to lie on her back. Support her lower legs with a cube placed under her knees. Now you have to stabilize the balance achieved in your client's body of light. Sit by your client's side and place one of your hands under her back where her kidneys are and place the other hand on her sole. Push life energy into your client from both sides until she feels increasing warmth and a flow from her legs into her lower back.

5. Do another assessment and compare to see if there are any differences between this and your first assessment. Ask your client if there is less pain and whether she experiences more flexibility in her movement. Record the changes in the symptoms before and after your treatment and compare them with the perceptions of changes you see in your client's life energy field. Make a record of these as well.

Prolapsed Disc

For the safety of your client as well as your own you should never treat a prolapsed disc without first seeing a radiological diagnosis. This will show you exactly where the problem is. Some forms of prolapsed discs may need surgery, for example, if there is any danger that a nerve will be destroyed or is causing

227

paralysis of the limbs, the bladder or the intestines. If the solid part of the destroyed disc narrows a nerve root, surgery may be necessary in some cases.

Avoid any kind of physical manipulation of the spine and be conscious of touching your client as gently as possible to ensure that you do not cause more harm. If you need to treat a prolapsed disc in the lumbar area ensure that your client is lying on the side where there is either no pain or less pain. If the prolapsed disc is in the cervical area place your client on their back.

Treating a prolapsed disc means improving the body's capacity to reabsorb the semi-fluid liquid found in the core of the disc which has leaked into the surrounding tissue causing the narrowing of nerve roots.

To reduce the inflammation and swelling and to relief the pain, use "cooler" colors such as light blue or indigo while you work with the "dissolving" technique. At the same time you also have to regenerate the irritated nerve roots, and stabilize the vertebrae against each other and relieve the tension of the muscles in the affected segment. In order to achieve good results in tissue regeneration you will have to work mainly with sound waves and the color red. To release muscular tension you will additionally have to use either the lower back or the neck and shoulder treatment and the kind you choose will depend on the area where the prolapsed disc is located.

Normally an acute prolapsed disc will take three to eight weeks to be sorted out. The use of hands-on healing will rapidly reduce the pain and improve your client's ability to move more easily in a significantly shorter period of time than usual. In an acute state, the treatment should be given at least three times a week. Between treatment sessions it will be very beneficial if your client has as much bed rest as possible. Physical strain or stress of any kind should be avoided.

The following is a guideline of how you could plan a whole treatment session for a client who is suffering from an acute prolapsed disc between the sixth and the seventh cervical vertebra. This guideline is not meant to be followed blindly. As a healer you have to be always aware that each individual client has specific needs and you may need to vary or change the techniques accordingly.

Do the following:
1. An Assessment
2. Local and Segmental Pain Relief
3. Tissue Regeneration
4. General Relaxation

Treating a Prolapsed Disc between the Sixth and the Seventh Cervical Vertebra

1. Assessment:
The client is a 37 year old woman suffering from severe pain in the neck which radiates into her left arm. She has a numb tickling sensation in her fingers. She is neither able to turn her head to the side nor bend it forward and back.

The radiological diagnosis indicates that she has a prolapsed disc between the sixth and the seventh vertebra. She does not have any ruptured cartilage parts of the disc which are pressing on the nerve root.

Treatment:
Sit behind your client and take the back of their head into your palms so that your fingertips lay at the base of the head and your client's ears are between your thumbs and your first finger. Gently pull life energy out of their cervical spine and check if there are any disturbances in the flow to the affected area. To improve your ability to perceive the body of light you

can do your assessment first and then later compare it to the medical diagnosis which will give you the perfect feedback.

2. To provide immediate pain relief, place your fingertips exactly on the area where you feel a disturbance in the flow. You will recognize a congestion of life energy which can be felt even on the physical level as increased tension in the muscles. Begin by dissolving it by using light blue or indigo. Ask your client for feedback and see if it corresponds with your perceptions of the changes that have occurred. In other words, do you feel the congestion dispersing and does your client feel less pain or no more pain and are the sensations in the fingers gone.

3. Now you can penetrate the whole area using sound waves and the color red. Be conscious of not putting too much pressure with your fingers against your client's neck. If the pain and the radiating sensations return, reduce the intensity of pushing in sound waves to a level at which these problems do not occur any more. After a while your client may experience a flow of warmth in her neck, arm and in some cases, along the whole spine.

4. Use the neck and shoulder treatment for general relaxation and complete the session by offering your client a glass of water.

Conclusion

When we think of the demographic distribution of population in Western Europe we find ourselves confronted with the fact that the percentage of older people will dramatically increase within the next twenty years. And among these older people will be your parents and yourself and your friends.

Using what you have learned about treating and preventing back problems in this book enables you to take an active role in supporting each other.

As the cost of medical treatment increases over the years you now have an effective tool to offer a viable cost effective alternative treatment. As a health professional specialized to treat back problems you are used to touching people with your hands and can easily incorporate the spine techniques described in this book into your work. If you are a massage therapist you will dramatically increase the therapeutic effects of a simple body massage using the hands-on healing techniques for the spine. This makes your work more efficient and will automatically lead to better results for your clients.

Prevention is better than cure, as the old saying goes. If you are setting out as a young person to practice the exercises in this book, you have a good chance of preventing back problems in the future. If you are an older person and are already suffering from some sort of back problems then you can start as of now to make your life better by practicing these exercises regularly. Besides getting rid of your back problems, exercising the spine in general will bring about many more benefits.

As soon as you understand that the spine is the central axis within the temple of your body you will discover that every part of your entire being is somehow connected to your spine. This is true for your physical as well as your emotional, mental and spiritual bodies. To balance them all together is the first requirement for the spiritual growth of your soul and the unfolding of your whole potential as a unique human being.

Bibliography

Bischof, Marco: *Biophotonen, Das Licht in unseren Zellen,* (Zweitausendeins 1995)

Bruyere, Rosalyn L.: *Wheels of Light,* (New York: Fireside, 1989)

Chia, Mantak: *Iron Shirt Chi Kung,* (Inner Traditions Bear and Company 2006)

Awaken Healing Energy Through the Tao, (Aurora Press 1991)

Dicke, Elisabeth: *Bindegewebsmassage,* (Hippokrates 1982)

Dvorak, Jiri: *Manuelle Medizin,* (Thieme 1988)

Feldenkrais, Moshe: *Awareness Through Movement,* (Harper Collins 1990)

Guttmann, Giselher: *Ich fühle, denke, träume und sterbe,* (Saur 1989)

Masters, Robert: *The Way To Awaken,* (Quest Books, 1997)

Storm, Hyemeyohsts: *Lightningbolt,* (Ballantine Books 1997)

Strotztka, Hans: *Psychotherapie und Tiefenpsychologie,* (Springer 1982)

Schwaller de Lubicz, R.A., *Sacred Sience,* (Inner Traditions 1998)

Schwegler, Johann S: *Der Mensch, Anatomie und Physiologie,* (Thieme 2006)

Wilson, Robert Anton: *Quantum Psychology,* (New Falcon 1990)

BOOKS

O is a symbol of the world, of oneness and unity. In different cultures it also means the "eye", symbolizing knowledge and insight. We aim to publish books that are accessible, constructive and that challenge accepted opinion, both that of academia and the "moral majority".

Our books are available in all good English language bookstores worldwide. If you don't see the book on the shelves ask the bookstore to order it for you, quoting the ISBN number and title. Alternatively you can order online (all major online retail sites carry our titles) or contact the distributor in the relevant country, listed on the copyright page.

See our website **www.o-books.net** for a full list of over 400 titles, growing by 100 a year.

And tune in to myspiritradio.com for our book review radio show, hosted by June-Elleni Laine, where you can listen to the authors discussing their books.

MySpiritRadio

SOME RECENT O BOOKS

An Exchange of Love
Madeleine Walker

A lovely book with a gentle and profound message about how closely our animal companions are linked to our triumphs and traumas, and an astonishing insight into how willing they are to be a surrogate for our stress symptoms and how instrumental they can be in our healing. Madeleine Walker is one of the best animal intuitives in the world.
Kindred Spirit

978-1-84694-139-9 186pp **£9.99 $19.95**

Colours of the Soul
June Mcleod

An excellent book! June Mcleod knows her subject extremely well. Comprehensive, it is jam-packed with excellent exercises. Definitely worth purchasing, there is something in this book for everyone. Pure magic!
Vision

1905047258 176pp **£11.99 $21.95**

Crystal Prescriptions
Judy Hall

Another potential best-seller from Judy Hall. This handy little book is packed as tight as a pill-bottle with crystal remedies for ailments. It is written in an easy-to-understand style, so if you are not a virtuoso with

your Vanadinite, it will guide you. If you love crystals and want to make the best use of them, it is worth investing in this book as a complete reference to their healing qualities.
Vision

1905047401 172pp **£7.99 $15.95**

Feng Shui Diaries
Richard Ashworth

This is no ordinary feng shui book. It is a vivid, sometimes touching, exploration of people's reasons, needs and motives for seeking change in their lives and a clever, novel way of portraying the far reaching scope of feng shui to professionals and lay people alike. Don't miss it.
Feng Shui News

1846940176 200pp **£9.99 $16.95**

Healing the Eternal Soul
Andy Tomlinson

Written with simple precision and sprinkled with ample case examples this will be an invaluable resource for those who assist others in achieving contact with the eternal part of themselves. It lends hope to those whose lives are 'stuck' or riddled with painful residuals from past lives. There are keys to open the doors to the transcendent knowledge of our Soul and the methods that Andy shares with us are those keys. This book is an invaluable contribution and advancement to the field of Regression Therapy. More so, it is an incredibly interesting read!
Dr Arthur E. Roffey, Past Vice-President, Society for Spiritual Regression

190504741X 192pp **£9.99 $19.95**

Passage to Freedom
A Path to Enlightenment
Dawn Mellowship

"Passage to Freedom" is an inspiring title that combines a spiritual treasure trove of wisdom with practical exercises accessible to all of us for use in our daily lives. Illustrated throughout with clear instructions, the information and inspiration emanating from Dawn Mellowship is a major achievement and will certainly help all readers gain insight into the way through and around life's problems, worries, and our own emotional, spiritual and physical difficulties.
Sandra Goodman PhD, Editor and Director, *Positive Health*

9781846940781 272pp £9.99 $22.95

Plant Spirit Wisdom
Sin Eaters and Shamans: The Power of Nature in Celtic Healing for the Soul
Ross Heaven

"The Joseph Campbell of our times".
James Shreeve, *Guardian* journalist

9781846941238 224pp £9.99 $19.95

Reiki Jin Kei Do
The Way of Compassion and Wisdom
Steve Gooch

This book is the first of its kind in Reiki in that it explores and challenges the origins and history of this therapy, and it would be a good read for

both the beginner and the more accomplished Reiki Master. This was a book I couldn't put down, and I think even those that don't feel a strong interest in Reiki itself would find this an interesting and informative read.
Choice Magazine

1905047851 240pp **£12.99 $21.95**

Reiki Meditations for Beginners
with free CD
Lawrence Ellyard

One of the few Reiki books which really covers something new and valuable. Reiki and Meditation is a core topic for everyone who likes to use Usui-Reiki as a spiritual path. This is why Mikao Usui emphasized so much to meditate every morning and every evening. A must read for every serious Reiki-Practitioner!
Walter Lübeck, co-author of The Spirit of Reiki

9781846940989 176pp **£12.99 $24.95**

Shamanic Reiki
Expanded Ways of Workling with Universal Life Force Energy
Llyn Roberts and Robert Levy

The alchemy of shamanism and Reiki is nothing less than pure gold in the hands of Llyn Roberts and Robert Levy. Shamanic Reiki brings the concept of energy healing to a whole new level. More than a how-to-book, it speaks to the health of the human spirit, a journey we must all complete.

Brian Luke Seaward, Ph.D., author of *Stand Like Mountain, Flow Like Water, Quiet Mind, Fearless Heart*
9781846940378 208pp £9.99 $19.95

The Essence of Reiki
The definitive guide to Usui Reiki
Dawn Mellowship and Andy Chrysostomou

Dawn and Andy are the first Reiki Masters in recent times to put forth the effort of restoring Reiki, a spiritual healing system promoting health and well being, towards the original goals and ideals of its founder Sensei Mikao Usui. This body of work inspires a new sense of spirituality that is currently deficient in the modern day worldwide Reiki community. Read this book to gain a deeper understanding of your Reiki practice, or let it inspire you to begin a new journey towards an incredible path of healing and self discovery for lifetimes to come.
Stephen Buck, Certified Massage Therapist, Reiki Master Teacher

9781846940996 240pp **£11.99 $24.95**

The Good Remembering
A Message for our Times
Llyn Roberts

Llyn's work changed my life. "The Good Remembering" is the most important book I've ever read.
John Perkins, *NY Times* best selling author of *Confessions of an Economic Hit Man*

1846940389 96pp **£7.99 $16.95**

The Healing Sourcebook
Discover your own path to better health and inner peace
David Vennells

Based on long experience of both receiving and giving healing treatments, it is useful to have so much information available in one book.
Network Review

1846940052 320pp **£14.99 $22.95**

Your Reiki Treatment
How to get the most out of it
Bronwen & Frans Stiene and Frans Stiene

Especially helpful and insightful. A down-to-earth book which can be recommended to Reaiki practitioners and clients alike. If you are new to reiki, then this is definitely THE book for you.
Mercury

1846940133 196pp **£9.99 $19.95**

Mysticism and Science
A Call for Reconciliation
Swami Abhayananda

A lucid and inspiring contribution to the great philosophical task of our age – the marriage of the perennial gnosis with modern science.
Timothy Freke author of *The Jesus Mysteries*

184694032X 144pp **£9.99 $19.95**

What a Body Knows
Finding Wisdom in Desire
Kimerer L. LaMothe PhD

I simply cannot praise the book enough! The prose is positively brilliant. It is full of sparkling gems of insight and astonishing, concise yet profound formulations. The nature passages remind me of Annie Dillard. It is truly a remarkable achievement!
Miranda Shaw, Ph.D., Professor of Religion, University of Richmond, Author of *Passionate Enlightenment: Women in Tantric Buddhism* and *Buddhist Goddesses of India*

978-1-84694-188-7 340pp **£11.99 $24.95**

Practicing Conscious Living and Dying
Stories of the Eternal Continuum of Consciousness
Annamaria Hemingway

This is a glorious book. A science of immortality is in the making, and Annamaria Hemingway is one of its architects.
Larry Dossey, MD, author of *The Extraordinary Healing Power of Ordinary Things*

9781846940774 224pp **£11.99 $24.95**

The Good Remembering
A Message for our Times
Llyn Roberts

Llyne's work changed my life. "The Good Remembering" is the most

important book I've ever read.
John Perkins, *NY Times* best selling author of *Confessions of an Economic Hit Man*

1846940389 96pp **£7.99 $16.95**

The Last Tourist in Iran
From Persepolis to Nuclear Natanz
Nicholas Hagger

The first book on Iran to combine travelogue with in-depth historical reflection/getting to the heart of the Iranian Islamic mind, this is a reflective look at the cultural heritage and present nuclear crisis in Iran – Iran's cultural and spiritual heritage is now threatened by policies that may trigger international intervention. Iran, a source of Western civilization, may be destroyed by its main beneficiary, Western civilization.

9781846940767 272pp **£11.99 $22.95**

The Author's Guide to Publishing and Marketing
Tim Ward and John Hunt

The inside story on how to get up the book sales ladder.

978-1-84694-166-5 224pp **£9.99 $19.95**